FRANK ROSIN
Modern GERMAN Cookbook

Modern
GERMAN
Cookbook

FRANK ROSIN

PHOTOGRAPHY: **KLAUS ARRAS**

CONTENTS

"The soul of a recipe
is the cooking,
and time is the best
ingredient.
We season by cooking,
not by seasoning."

Frank Rosin

COOKING WITH
PASSION

Germany's location—right in the heart of modern Europe—is reflected in our favorite dishes. These not only include well-known classics like beef roulades and Königsberg veal dumplings, but also pizza and pasta, döner kebabs, and gyros. Immigrants from southern and eastern Europe brought their family recipes and cooking traditions with them to the country, and the traditional and the modern blended in German cuisine over time. Modern German cuisine is vibrant and exciting, and it doesn't just draw from regional German cuisines. Today's cooking traditions are influenced by recipes and products from all over the world—a world that is rapidly shrinking thanks to mass travel and the internet.

With this cookbook, I give all those who love to cook recipes that have been tested and interpreted in the modern German style. Readers can alter recipes to suit themselves and then pass them on to others, because cooking traditions die without families to cook and enjoy meals together. It used to be that children learned to cook at home simply by watching. Today, it's unfortunate that we need cooking schools to teach us how to cook. I would love to change this trend, in what little way I can.

Great cooking is about passion. We shouldn't be too dogmatic in our approach to cooking, but rather work somewhat intuitively and instinctively. Good food satisfies essential basic needs and has such a great impact on our quality of life. That's why I recommend only cooking when you're hungry—a full stomach doesn't offer the taste buds sound advice.

Above all, don't deny yourself the pleasure of cooking by expecting perfection every time or being too hard on yourself over minor mistakes and mishaps. Stand at your stove and experience the passion of cooking, not with grim seriousness, but with gusto, and take it all with a pinch of salt. Here, I'll let my favorite quote from British chef Marco Pierre White guide you: "At the end of the day it's just food, isn't it? Just food." So, enjoy the cooking and the food!

Yours,
Frank Rosin

A huge thanks goes out to my executive chef, Oliver Engelke, and to my sous-chef, Christian Danielek, for their invaluable contributions to this cookbook.

THE RECIPES

The recipes in this book are divided into six chapters, reflecting the classic courses on a menu. This gives you the option of putting together a menu with several courses or combining different dishes to make a simple meal. It all depends on your preference.

In "Appetizers and Light Bites," the dishes range from Bavarian sausage salad with herbs, to beluga lentils with pernod, to buttery spinach gnocchi with parmesan cheese. Soups, featured in the next chapter, are an integral part of both traditional and modern German cuisine. Here you'll find diverse recipes such as classic wedding soup with cauliflower, foamed garlic soup with white wine, and tomato tea with bouquet garni.

The preparation of meat and poultry form the foundation of the German cooking tradition. Today, however, we happily forgo the heavy sauces of old. Roast beef with eggplant caviar and tomato salsa, leg of rabbit with potatoes and bell peppers, and curry wurst in fruit sauce are modern, light dishes. Traditional classics are represented too: sauerbraten, pan-fried veal in white wine sauce, and pork schnitzel in herb breading.

Germany does not have a long coastline, which explains why the chapter on fish is shorter than the others. Still, the recipes for trout, walleye, salmon, cod, and pickled herring will delight fish lovers. And the steamed monkfish ravioli with Asian vegetables is sure to convert even the last fish naysayer.

By comparison, the chapter on side dishes is particularly long, showcasing the wide variety of side dishes that is typically German. Dumplings, spätzle, and Swabian potato noodles, just like vegetables, are valued as accompaniments to fish and meat. When combined, several sides can be served as a main course or as appetizers. I've also thrown in some unusual dishes, such as layered potato cake and fried rice balls.

Hot and cold desserts round out the recipe chapters—cherry parfait with lemongrass, warm peaches in parchment paper, or semolina pudding with marinated plums will transport you to dessert heaven.

Last, but not least, I've provided basic recipes for broth, mayonnaise, and salad dressings that taste infinitely better than anything you'll buy in the supermarket.

In cooking, use the best quality products, and, where possible, use local products, since the dishes are often simple and benefit immeasurably from the quality and freshness of the ingredients. If lemon zest is needed, always try to buy organic lemons that have not been sprayed with pesticides.

A remark about the cooling times listed in the recipes that use gelatin: Because refrigerators, room temperature, and ingredients influence the gelling process, the times given are approximate, based on my experience. And, too, the cooking times given are usually approximate, since the cooking time needed always depends on the ingredients in the recipe.

For the most part, these recipes are not aimed at beginners, so I started with the assumption that the reader would be working in a well-equipped kitchen. Indispensable items in a stocked kitchen include a large ovenproof frying pan, a food processor with a blender, or a powerful electric hand mixer and a handheld blender. A juicer and an iSi-Whip for foaming also are very useful. For a few dishes, you will need heatproof plastic wrap or aluminum foil.

Now that you're equipped with these recipes, nothing stands between you and cooking pleasure. Enjoy your journey through the fascinating world of modern German cuisine!

ROSIN'S
RULES

These simple ground rules form the core of my cooking theory
and they are the basis of good cooking. All the recipes in this
book—in fact, all of my recipes—are built around these principles.

> **Time** is the most important ingredient.

> **Concentrate and reduce**
to build and enhance flavor.

> **Never season wildly**—this
kills the character and subtlety of ingredients.

> **Salt and sugar** belong together.

> **Caramelizing** brings out original flavors
and taste.

> **Acidity** should be used deliberately **as a
counterbalance** to sweetness.

> **Cooking water** should be **seasoned**, just
like poaching liquid, so that it imparts flavor to
ingredients rather than robbing them of flavor.

APPETIZERS
AND LIGHT BITES

BUTTERY **SPINACH GNOCCHI** WITH PARMESAN CHEESE

This classic recipe originated in Italy and was adopted here in Germany. Simple and delicious, this dish is one of my favorites.

> **serves 4–6**
> **25 minutes**

1lb 8oz (700g) spinach
4oz (120g) Parmesan cheese
1 shallot
1 garlic clove
salt
4 eggs
2 tbsp bread crumbs
2 tbsp olive oil
sugar
freshly ground black pepper
freshly grated nutmeg
2–3 tbsp unsalted butter
lemon juice
red pepper flakes

1 Coarsely tear the spinach leaves, removing the stems. Grate the Parmesan cheese. Peel and dice the shallot and garlic. In a medium saucepan, bring salted water to a boil. Pour boiling water over the spinach and blanch for 1 minute. Drain well. Cut the spinach into thin strips and place it in a bowl. Add the eggs, 2½oz (70g) of the Parmesan cheese, and the bread crumbs. Combine well.

2 Heat 1 tablespoon of olive oil in a frying pan. Add the shallot and garlic and sauté until translucent. Season to taste with sugar and salt. Add to the spinach mixture and combine thoroughly. Season to taste with salt, pepper, and nutmeg.

3 Using two tablespoons, shape 12 large gnocchi from the mixture. Heat the butter in a frying pan. Add the gnocchi and fry for 5–7 minutes on both sides, until golden brown. Remove them from the pan and drain on paper towels. Divide the gnocchi among plates, then sprinkle with the remaining Parmesan. Drizzle with the remaining olive oil and a squeeze of lemon juice. Sprinkle red pepper flakes on top, to taste. Serve immediately.

ROSIN'S TIP: Spinach gnocchi are usually cooked gently in barely simmering water. Frying them slowly in butter deepens the flavor of the gnocchi and intensifies the spinach taste.

SWEET AND SOUR
CUCUMBER SALAD
WITH SALMON TARTAR

For me, this is the best cucumber salad in the world! I created the recipe 22 years ago in an emergency and have been tweaking and improving it ever since. It's now become a permanent fixture in my recipe collection.

> serves 4–6
> 35 minutes + 2 hours to marinate

1 Cut the cucumbers in half lengthwise, then seed and dice them. Peel and chop the ginger and garlic. Peel and dice the onions. Heat 1 tablespoon of olive oil in a frying pan. Add the onions and garlic and sauté until translucent. Remove from the heat.

2 Cut the salmon fillet into thin strips, then finely dice the strips. Place the salmon in a bowl, add the cilantro and ginger, and combine. Season to taste with salt and pepper. Stir in half of the cooked onion and garlic. Place the bowl in the refrigerator.

3 Combine the cucumbers and remaining onion and garlic. Add the sweet chili sauce, mustard, curry powder, sugar, dill, vinegar, and ⅓ cup of olive oil. Stir to combine. Marinate in the refrigerator for at least 2 hours.

4 Season the cucumber salad to taste with salt, pepper, and vinegar. Divide the salad among glass jars, then arrange the salmon tartar on top. Garnish with dill fronds. Serve immediately.

2 English cucumbers
¾in (2cm) fresh ginger
1 garlic clove
2 onions
⅓ cup, plus 1 tbsp olive oil
6oz (170g) boneless, skinless salmon fillet
1 tsp finely chopped cilantro
salt
freshly ground black pepper
¾ cup sweet chili sauce
1 tsp mustard
1 tsp curry powder
1 tbsp sugar
1 tbsp dill, finely chopped
⅔ cup white wine vinegar
dill fronds, to garnish

 ROSIN'S TIP: Cucumbers are 90 percent water, so this salad really benefits when you salt the cucumbers once the seeds have been removed. After salting, place the cucumbers in a sieve and drain for 45 minutes. This enhances flavor and keeps the dressing from becoming watery.

ONION TART
WITH WESTPHALIAN HAM

When I invite friends over to watch soccer matches, I serve this tart and pair it with cold beer. It goes just as well with a crisp white wine at a girls' get-together. For a twist, substitute leeks for the onions.

> serves 4–6
> 1 hour 20 minutes + 7 hours to dry and cool

6 thick slices Westphalian ham, or a dry cured ham such as prosciutto
1½ cups all-purpose flour
9 tbsp unsalted butter, chilled and cut into cubes
8 eggs
salt
2lb 4oz (1kg) onions
2 tbsp canola oil
¼ cup white wine
1 tbsp thyme leaves, finely chopped
freshly ground black pepper
1¼ cups fresh cheese, such as quark or ricotta, or sour cream

1 Preheat a convection oven to 175°F (80°C) or a conventional oven to 200°F (95°C). Place the ham on a baking sheet lined with parchment paper. Dry in the oven overnight, or for at least 6 hours. Cool for 1 hour, then cut into thin strips.

2 Combine the flour, butter, 2 eggs, and a pinch of salt to make a smooth dough. Roll the dough into a ball, wrap it in plastic wrap, and refrigerate for at least 1 hour.

3 Preheat a convection oven to 350°F (170°C) or a conventional oven to 375°F (185°C). Peel and slice the onions. Heat the oil in a large frying pan, add the onions, and sauté until translucent. Pour in the wine and cook until the liquid has evaporated. Season with thyme, salt, and pepper. Add the ham and combine.

Meanwhile, roll out the dough to fit a 6 × 6in (15 × 15cm) jelly roll pan. Make an edge 1in (2.5cm) high. Blind bake the dough on the center rack of the oven for 15 minutes (see below).

4 Take the pie crust from the oven, and remove the baking beans and parchment paper. Distribute the onion mixture evenly over the pie crust. Reduce the oven temperature to 250°F (120°C) for a convection oven or to 275°F (135°C) for a conventional oven. Whisk together the cheese and the remaining 6 eggs. Pour the mixture over the onions, making sure the liquid does not seep under the crust. Bake on the center rack for 40 minutes, until the egg has set. Remove the tart from the oven. Let cool. Cut into squares to serve.

ROSIN'S TIP: Blind baking produces a flaky crust. To blind bake, place parchment paper on the unbaked pie crust and fill it with dried beans. The weight of the beans keeps the crust from bubbling up during baking and prevents air bubbles from forming.

LAMB'S LETTUCE WITH BACON, MUSHROOMS, AND CROUTONS

Served with a crisp white wine, this simple salad makes a perfect light summer lunch. Top each salad with half a hard-boiled egg if you like.

> serves 4–6
> 35 minutes

1 Wash the lettuce and place it in a bowl. Using a sharp knife, remove the skin from the mushrooms. Cut off the stems and gills and slice the mushrooms in half. Remove the bread crusts, then cut the bread into ½in (1.5cm) cubes. Finely chop the parsley leaves, discarding the stems.

2 Heat 1 tablespoon of olive oil in a frying pan. Add the bread cubes and fry until golden brown. Remove the pan from the heat, stir in the parsley, and season to taste with salt and pepper.

Transfer to a plate to cool. Return the frying pan to the stove. Add the remaining olive oil and the bacon to the pan and fry the bacon over medium heat until crisp. Drain on paper towels.

3 Prepare the Champagne dressing. Pour it over the lettuce and toss. Divide the lettuce among 4 bowls. Arrange the mushrooms, croutons, and bacon on top. Serve immediately.

8oz (225g) lamb's lettuce
9oz (250g) button mushrooms
3 slices white bread
1 bunch of parsley
sea salt
freshly ground black pepper
8 slices bacon
2 tbsp olive oil

CHAMPAGNE DRESSING
(see page 217)

 ROSIN'S TIP: If you want to save on prep time, you can cut the mushrooms into thin slices. Take the time to remove the skin and gills, however, since this will enhance the flavor of the mushrooms.

PURÉED BREAD
AND MUSSELS

While traveling in Portugal, I came to appreciate Portuguese cuisine at the *Herdade dos Grous* vineyard in Alentejo. It was there that I was served a typical poor-man's meal that was so fantastic it prompted me to "translate" it into German.

> **serves 4–6**
> **1½ hours**

2 tbsp olive oil
6 garlic cloves
1 onion
1 carrot
1 celery stalk
4 cups white wine
2 sprigs of thyme
2 bay leaves
10 peppercorns
1 tbsp chopped fresh ginger
⅔ cup Pernod
salt
sugar
10½oz (300g) mussels
10 slices day-old white bread
1 tbsp chopped cilantro
lemon juice

1 Heat 1 tablespoon of olive oil in a saucepan. Peel and chop the garlic cloves and sauté them in the oil. Coarsely chop the onion, carrot, and celery. Add the vegetables to the saucepan and sauté, stirring constantly. Deglaze with the wine and 2 cups of water. Add the thyme, bay leaves, peppercorns, and ginger. Reduce the liquid by two-thirds.

2 Season the liquid to taste with the Pernod, salt, and sugar. Wash the mussels well under cold running water. Place them in the saucepan, return the poaching liquid to a boil, and boil for 5 minutes. Place a sieve over a second saucepan. Strain the mussels and their liquid into the saucepan and put it on the stove. Boil the cooking liquid over medium heat until it is reduced to ¾ cup. Remove the mussels from their shells.

3 Cut the bread into cubes, place them in a saucepan, and add the cooking liquid. Stir well, until no more pieces of bread are visible, then fold in the mussels. Season to taste with the remaining olive oil, the cilantro, and the lemon juice. Serve immediately.

ROSIN'S TIP: If you want to serve puréed bread as a side dish, but don't have time to make cooking liquid from scratch, substitute ¾ cup of fish stock. In this case, the final seasoning with olive oil, cilantro, and lemon juice is especially important.

CRISPY **BLOOD SAUSAGE STRUDELS** WITH A MEDITERRANEAN TOUCH

Chef Alfons Schuhbeck made this dish at my restaurant in 1994. It is simple, delicious, and creative. I have adapted his recipe, making the flavor of my version slightly milder than the original. You don't have to make the phyllo dough yourself: store-bought dough works just as well.

> › serves 4–6
> › 35 minutes + 4½ hours to refrigerate

1 Place the apple juice and lemon juice in a saucepan. Bring to a boil, then remove from the heat. Sprinkle gelatin over the liquid and let it dissolve. Cool the apple jelly for 4 hours, until set.

2 Peel and dice the shallot and garlic. Heat the olive oil in a frying pan, add the shallot and garlic, and sauté until translucent. Season to taste with the sugar and salt. Remove from the heat and transfer to a bowl.

3 Finely chop the thyme and marjoram leaves. Peel, quarter, and core the apple. Cut the apple into ¼in (5mm) cubes. Remove the sausage casing. Cut the sausage and the apple jelly into ¼in (5mm) cubes. Add these ingredients to the bowl with the shallot and garlic and combine. Season to taste with salt, then let cool for 30 minutes.

4 Preheat a convection oven to 350°F (180°C) or a conventional oven to 375°F (190°C). Line a baking sheet with parchment paper. Melt the butter. Arrange the two pieces of dough on top of each other. Cut into four pieces. Brush with melted butter. Place 2 tablespoons of sausage filling in the center of each piece of dough, fold the dough in from the sides, and roll to enclose the filling. Brush with melted butter as you go. Place the strudels on the baking sheet and bake on the center rack of the oven for 15–18 minutes, until golden brown. Serve warm.

¾ cup apple juice
1 sqeeze of lemon juice
1 tbsp unflavored powered gelatin
1 shallot
1 garlic clove
1 tbsp olive oil
sugar
1 pinch of salt
1 bunch of thyme leaves
1 bunch of marjoram leaves
1 apple
10½oz (300g) blood sausage
7 tbsp unsalted butter
2 sheets of phyllo dough

 ROSIN'S TIP: Strudel is surprisingly tasty with fried fish. Brush the dough with melted butter so it cooks evenly. I fry the strudels for a few minutes, then bake them for 10 minutes. The dough becomes extra crispy—a lovely contrast to the soft filling.

WHEAT BERRIES WITH SUMMER VEGETABLES AND ROSÉ WINE

Here's a truly tasty vegetarian dish that even meat-lovers will enjoy—I eat it nearly every week. Grains have always been important in German cooking, and, despite the Mediterranean ingredients, this recipe is typically German.

> serves 4–6
> 1 hour

14oz (400g) wheat berries, about 2½ cups
1 tsp salt
2 red bell peppers
1 zucchini
2 shallots
1 garlic clove
1 jalapeño pepper
3½oz (100g) Parmesan cheese
3–4 tbsp olive oil
freshly ground black pepper
sugar
1 tbsp tomato paste
10 cherry tomatoes
1 cup vegetable stock
½ cup rosé wine
2 tbsp lemon juice
1 tbsp thyme leaves

1 Rinse the wheat berries and place them in a saucepan. Add 5 cups of water and the salt and bring to a boil. Reduce the heat and simmer for 1 hour, or until the berries are tender. Drain the wheat berries in a sieve.

2 While the wheat berries are cooking, remove the seeds and pith from the bell peppers. Cut the bell peppers and zucchini into ¼in (5mm) dice. Peel and dice the shallots and garlic. Slice off the bottom third of the jalapeño, remove the seeds, and cut it into thin strips. Using a vegetable peeler, shave the Parmesan cheese.

3 Heat 2 tablespoons of olive oil in a frying pan. Add the vegetables and sauté. Season to taste with salt, pepper, and sugar. Stir in the tomato paste and cherry tomatoes and continue to sauté. Add the stock and wine.

4 Place the cooked wheat berries in the frying pan and stir well to combine. Remove from the heat. Season to taste with lemon juice, thyme, and the remaining olive oil. Divide the wheat berries among bowls and sprinkle with the shaved Parmesan. Serve.

ROSIN'S TIP: For a spicier take on this recipe, add 2 bay leaves, 2 cloves, and 1 pinch of curry powder to the berries while they are cooking.

FARMER'S SALAD WITH FETA CHEESE AND DRIED TOMATOES

The cooking traditions of Italy, Spain, Turkey, and other Mediterranean countries have influenced German cuisine in the past few decades, as can be seen in this recipe. This farmer's salad is a must-have at a barbeque, and it also makes an ideal accompaniment to pan-fried meat.

> serves 4–6
> 20 minutes + 30 minutes to marinate

1 Clean, then slice the mushrooms. Seed the peppers and cut them into ½in (1cm) cubes. Cut the celery into ½in (1cm) pieces and halve the cherry tomatoes. Finely dice the dried tomatoes. Peel and slice the onions.

2 Heat 1 tablespoon of olive oil in a frying pan. Add the mushrooms and sauté over high heat. Remove from the heat and place in a salad bowl. Season to taste with herbed salt, pepper, and sugar. Stir in the remaining prepared ingredients. Season to taste with olive oil and distilled vinegar. Marinate in the refrigerator for 30 minutes. Cut the Feta cheese into cubes or crumble it into little pieces. Scatter the cheese and parsley over the top. Serve immediately.

3½oz (100g) crimini mushrooms
1 small red bell pepper
1 small yellow bell pepper
1 stalk celery
10 cherry tomatoes
½ cup sun-dried tomatoes in oil
2 red onions
2–3 tbsp olive oil
herbed salt (see page 219)
freshly ground black pepper
sugar
distilled vinegar
7oz (200g) Feta cheese
1 tbsp chopped parsley, to garnish

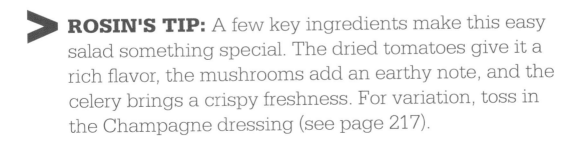

ROSIN'S TIP: A few key ingredients make this easy salad something special. The dried tomatoes give it a rich flavor, the mushrooms add an earthy note, and the celery brings a crispy freshness. For variation, toss in the Champagne dressing (see page 217).

BELUGA LENTILS
WITH PERNOD

Lentils are incredibly versatile: they are delicious in appetizers and hearty soups. By doubling this recipe and serving it with veal patties (see page 44), you have the makings of a wonderful main course.

> serves 4–6
> 35 minutes

6 garlic cloves
1 sprig of rosemary
1 sprig of thyme
6 star anise
1 cup beluga lentils
4 shallots
2–3 tbsp olive oil
2 tbsp sugar
¾ cup balsamic vinegar
¾ cup vegetable stock
salt
freshly ground black pepper
1 splash of Pernod

1 Place 2 garlic cloves, the rosemary and thyme, and the star anise in a paper tea filter. Make a bouquet garni by tying the filter with kitchen twine. Put the lentils, 2½ cups water, and the bouquet garni in a saucepan and bring to a boil. Cook the lentils over medium heat for 15 minutes, until firm to the bite. Remove from the heat, drain, and cool under cold running water.

2 While the lentils are cooking, peel and dice the remaining garlic cloves and the shallots. Heat 1 tablespoon of olive oil in a frying pan. Add the shallots and garlic and sauté until translucent. Stir in the sugar until caramelized. Deglaze with the balsamic vinegar. Reduce the liquid until it is syrupy. Pour in the stock and add the lentils. Season to taste with salt, pepper, olive oil, and Pernod. Spoon the lentils into small jars. Serve.

ROSIN'S TIP: Bouquets garni are ideal for adding flavor to stews, soups, and sauces because the herbs can be removed easily from the pan. Paper filters are good for one-time use, while linen and cotton bags can be reused.

BAVARIAN SAUSAGE SALAD WITH HERBS

Purists may disagree with me, but I like to eat this salad with homemade mayonnaise (see page 218). The combination is simply delicious.

> **serves 4–6**
> **30 minutes + 6 hours to marinate**

1 Preheat the oven to 350°F (180°C). Place the leberkäse on a baking sheet. Bake on the center rack of the oven for 10–15 minutes, until the sausage turns a lovely golden-brown color. Remove and let cool.

2 Meanwhile, cut the dill pickles and radishes into thin strips. Peel and finely slice the shallots. Dice the white part of the scallions, discarding the remainder.

3 Cut the cooled leberkäse into thin strips. Place the sausage in a bowl along with the dill pickles, radishes, shallots, and scallions. Season to taste with salt, pepper, distilled vinegar, and canola oil. Place the salad in the refrigerator for 6 hours to marinate.

4 Chop the chervil and parsley. Season the salad again to taste, then mix in the herbs. Serve immediately.

1lb 5oz (600g) loaf leberkäse
2 large dill pickles
4 radishes
2 shallots
2 scallions
 salt
freshly ground black pepper
distilled vinegar
canola oil
1 bunch of chervil
1 bunch of parsley

 ROSIN'S TIP: Leberkäse is a Bavarian meatloaf made from finely ground pork sausage. Browning it in the oven gives the meat a delicious roasted flavor. If leberkäse is not readily available in your area, you can use mortadella sausage instead.

VEAL IN ASPIC WITH WARM REMOULADE FOAM

Careful layering is necessary when making this jellied veal dish. The vegetables must be smoothed flat and pressed down firmly before being topped with the next slice of veal.

> **serves 4**
> **50 minutes + 5½ hours to cook and cool**

3 garlic cloves
lemon
8½ cups veal or beef stock
1 tbsp caraway seeds
1lb 2oz (500g) boneless veal eye round
1½ tbsp unflavored powdered gelatin
sea salt
freshly ground black pepper
1 bunch of thyme leaves
1 bunch of chervil leaves
2 carrots
1 shallot
½ head of celery root
1 large zucchini
1 tbsp canola oil
sugar

REMOULADE FOAM
(see page 218)

1 Peel 2 garlic cloves and cut the lemon in quarters. Place the stock, garlic, lemon, and caraway seeds in a saucepan. Bring to a boil, add the veal, and boil for 1½ hours. Take the saucepan off the stove, remove the meat from the stock, and let cool. Ladle 2 cups of stock into a second saucepan and bring to a boil. Sprinkle the gelatin over the hot stock and stir to dissolve. Season to taste and let cool. Cut the veal into ¼in (5mm) slices. Cut 16 pieces from the veal, each 2in (5cm) round.

2 Finely chop the thyme and chervil. Peel and dice the carrots, shallot, celery root, and remaining garlic clove. Dice the zucchini. Heat the canola oil in a frying pan. Add the shallots, garlic, carrots, and celery root. Sauté until the shallots are translucent. Add the zucchini and cook until tender. Season to taste with salt, pepper, sugar, chervil, and thyme. Remove from the heat.

3 Line four 2in (5cm) dessert molds with plastic wrap, covering the bottoms and sides. Place a ½in- (1 cm-) thick slice of veal in each mold. Put a ½in (1 cm) layer of vegetables on top of the veal. Repeat twice, until the vegetables are used up. Top with 1 slice of veal. Pour the now cold stock into the molds. Refrigerate for 4 hours.

4 Using a sharp knife, carefully loosen the aspics from the molds. Turn onto plates. Peel off the plastic wrap. Serve with warm remoulade foam.

ROSIN'S TIP:
If you prefer, you can use chicken instead of veal. To give the aspic a rich flavor, you will need a hearty stock, such as the broth from the roast beef recipe on page 80.

34

SMOKED SALMON AND CHEESE ON PUMPERNICKEL

This recipe requires some advance prep work, so give yourself plenty of time when making it. It's great party fare, and the salmon log can be assembled a day ahead and refrigerated. Put the log in the freezer before slicing it.

> **serves 4**
> **25 minutes + 3 hours to refrigerate**

1 Finely chop the chervil. Place the gelatin in a small bowl. Add 2 tablespoons boiling water and stir to dissolve. Stir the chervil into the fresh cheese. Season to taste with salt, pepper, and lemon juice. Gradually add the cheese to the dissolved gelatin. Place the bowl in the refrigerator for 2 hours, until the cheese becomes firm.

2 Lay the salmon slices side by side. Spread the cheese evenly down the middle of the salmon. Roll into a firm log 1in (2.5cm) in diameter. Put the log in the freezer for 1 hour.

3 Cut 8 rounds, each 1in (2.5cm) in diameter, from the pumpernickel bread. Remove the salmon log from the freezer, take off the plastic wrap, and cut the log into 8 equal slices. Place the slices on the pumpernickel bread and arrange on plates. Garnish with dill and serve.

½ bunch of chervil
1½ tbsp unflavored powdered gelatin
14oz (400g) fresh cheese, such as ricotta, quark, mascarpone, or cream cheese
salt
freshly ground black pepper
lemon juice
8 slices smoked salmon
4 slices pumpernickel bread
1 tsp chopped dill

 ROSIN'S TIP: To roll the salmon without damaging the outside layer, lay it on plastic wrap and use the plastic wrap to roll the fish and filling into a log.

FENNEL AND ORANGE SALAD WITH SMOKED TROUT

Carmelization is what gives this dish its special flair. The subtle flavor of the melted sugar marries the sweetness of the orange with the freshness of the fennel.

> **serves 4**
> **30 minutes**

4 tbsp unsalted butter
¼ cup vegetable stock
1 bay leaf
4 smoked trout fillets, about
   3oz (85g) each
3 oranges
2 heads of fennel
2 shallots
1 garlic clove
1 tbsp olive oil
2 tbsp sugar
1 bunch of thyme leaves
½ cup dry white wine
salt
freshly ground black pepper

1 Heat the butter, stock, and bay leaf in a frying pan over low heat. Add the smoked trout fillets to warm them. Squeeze the juice of 1 orange and cut the segments from the remaining 2 oranges. Set aside.

2 Quarter and core the fennel, then slice it into thin strips. Peel the shallots and slice them into strips. Peel and chop the garlic. Heat the olive oil in a frying pan. Add the fennel, shallots, and garlic, and sauté for 3 minutes.

Add the sugar and thyme leaves and stir. Deglaze with the orange juice and white wine. Remove from the heat and strain, reserving the cooking liquid.

3 Return the liquid to the frying pan. Let boil until the liquid has almost evaporated and the sugar has begun to caramelize. Add the orange segments. Fold in the fennel. Toss well and season with salt and pepper. Serve the trout fillets topped with the salad.

ROSIN'S TIP: Don't heat the trout for too long because it will continue to cook as it cools. You can also serve the smoked trout cold.

ROSIN'S TIP:

For a bit of variety, swap Belgian endive for the Boston lettuce. And instead of using tiny North Atlantic shrimp, make the recipe with lobster or jumbo shrimp. The cocktail sauce also works well as a salad dressing or vegetable dip.

SHRIMP COCKTAIL
WITH A FRUITY SALAD

In the 1970s, shrimp cocktail was an elegant appetizer and extremely popular with the so-called "Jet Set." Proper style called for arranging the shrimp on top of finely sliced hearts of Boston lettuce and serving the dish in wide Champagne glasses. This recipe—including the canned peaches—is a nod to that era.

> **serves 4**
> **20 minutes**

1 Peel and dice the shallot and garlic. Heat the oil in a frying pan. Add the shallot, garlic, and sugar. Sauté over low heat until translucent. Remove from the heat.

2 Quarter the head of lettuce, remove the core, and slice each quarter into thin strips. Place the lettuce in a bowl and stir in the shallots and garlic. Put in a cool place. Dice the peaches and mix them into the salad.

3 Put the mayonnaise in a bowl, add the tomato paste, cognac, and lemon juice, and combine well. Season to taste with salt and cayenne pepper. Add the shrimp to the cocktail sauce and toss. To serve, arrange the shrimp salad and the lettuce in glass jars or on plates.

1 shallot
1 garlic clove
1 tbsp canola oil
1 tbsp sugar
1 head of Boston lettuce
4 peach halves (from the can)
½ cup mayonnaise (see page 218)
3 tbsp tomato paste
1 splash of cognac
2 tbsp lemon juice
salt
cayenne pepper
14oz (400g) cooked small North Atlantic or Maine shrimp, peeled

MUSHROOM-TOPPED
POTATO AND
VEGETABLE PANCAKES

Vegetarians will love these hearty little pancakes. Serve them as appetizers, sides, or even as a small main course. Make sure to squeeze all the liquid from the potatoes, so they fry up crisp, not soggy.

> serves 4
> 1 hour

1lb 12oz (800g) Russet
    Burbank potatoes
14oz (400g) crimini mushrooms
1 shallot
1 carrot
¼ head of celery root
½ leek
3 tbsp olive oil
salt and freshly ground
    black pepper
sugar
½ cup dry white wine
⅓ cup crème fraîche
2 egg yolks
freshly grated nutmeg
1 tbsp chives, finely chopped,
    to garnish

1 Peel and grate the potatoes. Clean and slice the mushrooms. Peel and dice the shallot. Cut the carrots, celery root, and leek into thin strips. Heat 1 tablespoon of olive oil in a frying pan. Add the mushrooms and sauté. Season to taste with salt, pepper, and sugar. Add the shallot and sweat. Deglaze with the wine, then add the crème fraîche. Simmer until the liquid has almost evaporated. Set aside and keep warm.

2 Using paper towels, squeeze the liquid from the potatoes and put them in a bowl. Add the egg yolks, carrots, celery root, and leek, and combine. Season with salt, pepper, and nutmeg.

3 Heat 1 tablespoon of olive oil in a large frying pan. Place 4 heaping tablespoons of the potato mixture side by side in the frying pan, leaving ample room between them. Press flat. Fry over medium heat on each side until golden brown. Remove the potato pancakes from the frying pan. Drain on paper towels. Heat the remaining olive oil, and fry 4 more potato pancakes. Remove from the pan and drain on paper towels. Place 1 potato pancake on each plate. Top each with mushrooms, cover with another potato pancake, and top again with mushrooms. Sprinkle with chives and serve immediately.

ROSIN'S TIP: Sauté onions, shallots, and garlic very gently, so that the liquid they contain evaporates and their sugars slowly caramelize. This reduces the sharpness of the vegetables, while enhancing their flavors.

BEET SALAD
WITH CELERY ROOT PURÉE

Beets have enjoyed a spectacular comeback in the past few years. It's no wonder—they have a wonderfully earthy taste and a subtle acidity. The combination of beets, puréed celery root, the roasted flavor of brown butter, and a dash of cayenne is incomparable. This vegetable dish is so ingenious, I guarantee you won't miss meat or fish.

> serves 4
> 50 minutes + 2 days to marinate

1 For the beet salad, peel and dice the shallot. Melt the butter in a saucepan, add the shallot, and sauté over medium heat until translucent. Meanwhile, cut the beets into large cubes. Add the cubes to the shallots and stir. Remove from the heat and transfer to a bowl. Let cool. In another bowl, combine the micro-greens, cilantro, and 1 teaspoon of chervil. Season with salt, pepper, and distilled vinegar. Stir into the beets. Cover and refrigerate for 2 days.

2 To make the celery root purée, peel and dice the celery root. Place 1¾ cups of stock and the celery root in a saucepan and bring to a boil. Simmer for 10 minutes, then strain through a sieve. Put 7 tablespoons of butter and the crème fraîche in a bowl and add the celery root. Purée with a handheld mixer. Season with salt, pepper, and sugar. Keep warm.

3 Put the remaining 9 tablespoons of butter into a saucepan and heat it until it no longer foams and browns. Strain through a fine-mesh sieve lined with a paper towels into a small metal bowl. Using a handheld mixer, blend the brown butter with the remaining stock and lemon juice. Season to taste with cayenne pepper.

4 Heat the oil in a deep fryer or saucepan. Use enough oil so the shallots float in the oil. Peel and dice the shallots. Combine with the flour, 1 pinch of salt, 1 teaspoon of sugar, and 1 pinch of cayenne pepper. Fry the shallots in the hot oil until crisp. Drain on paper towels.

5 Place the purée into bowls and top with the beets. Drizzle with the brown butter. Garnish with shallots and 1 teaspoon of chervil. Serve immediately.

BEET SALAD
1 shallot
4 tbsp unsalted butter
4 peeled, cooked beets
2 cups mixed micro-greens
2 tsp chopped cilantro leaves
2 tsp chopped chervil leaves
salt and freshly ground black pepper
2 tbsp distilled vinegar

CELERY ROOT PURÉE
2 heads of celery root
2 cups vegetable stock
16 tbsp unsalted butter, softened
¼ cup crème fraîche
salt and freshly ground black pepper
sugar
juice of 1 lemon
cayenne pepper
canola oil, for frying
6 shallots
2 tbsp all-purpose flour

 ROSIN'S TIP: Some of the beets' acidity is lost in marination, so add a dash of distilled vinegar before serving the beets. Distilled vinegar is stronger than white wine vinegar, yet flavorless.

POTATO SALAD
WITH CAPER-AND-ROSEMARY VEAL PATTIES

This potato salad was always available at my mother's French-fry stand—and it was always a best-seller. Serve the potato salad with these delicious veal patties and a simple dish becomes a special meal.

> serves 6
> 1 hour 15 minutes + 5 hours to marinate

POTATO SALAD
1lb 2oz (500g) Yukon Gold
   potatoes
2 bay leaves
1 teaspoon caraway seeds
salt
6 eggs
2 large dill pickles
2 shallots
1 cup mayonnaise (see
   page 218)
dill pickle liquid, from the jar
freshly ground black pepper
1 bunch of chives

VEAL PATTIES
2 day-old bread rolls
1 splash of milk
3 shallots
1 bunch of rosemary leaves
¼ cup capers
2lb 4oz (1kg) ground veal
3 tbsp canola oil
2 eggs
2 tbsp mustard
salt and freshly ground black
   pepper

1 Place the potatoes in a large saucepan. Add bay leaves and caraway seeds. Cover with cold water and season generously with salt. Bring to a boil. Cook the potatoes for 20 minutes, or until tender. Drain the potatoes, let them cool, and peel. Place the eggs in boiling water and cook for 12 minutes, until hard-boiled. Peel the eggs. Coarsely chop the eggs and dill pickles. Peel and dice the shallots. Cut the potatoes into thin slices.

2 Place the prepared ingredients in a bowl. Combine with the homemade mayonnaise. Season to taste with dill pickle liquid, salt, and pepper. Place the salad in the refrigerator to marinate overnight, or for at least 5 hours. Chop the chives finely, add them to the potato salad, and combine thoroughly. Season again with salt, pepper, and dill pickle liquid.

3 To make the veal patties, cut the bread rolls into small pieces and soak in the milk for 20 minutes. Peel and dice the shallots. Finely chop the rosemary and capers. Place the ground meat in a bowl. Heat 1 tablespoon of the oil in a frying pan, add the shallots, and sauté until translucent. Squeeze the bread well to remove the liquid. Add the bread, shallots, eggs, mustard, rosemary, and capers to the ground veal, then combine thoroughly. Season with salt and pepper.

4 In a large frying pan, heat the remaining oil. Shape 12 patties from the ground meat and fry over medium heat on both sides, until golden brown. Serve the veal patties with the potato salad on the side.

ROSIN'S TIP: Adding caraway seeds and bay leaf to the cooking water makes the boiled potatoes more flavorful.

SOUPS

WEDDING SOUP
WITH CAULIFLOWER

Soup is the classic first course in German cuisine, which explains why we have so many soup recipes. This wedding soup is the quintessential German soup.

> serves 4
> 45 minutes + 1 hour to cool

2 large eggs
2 large egg yolks
salt
freshly grated nutmeg
¾ cup milk
1 tsp softened unsalted butter
5¼ cups beef stock
4 spears of white asparagus
½ head of cauliflower, cut into florets
1 tbsp chopped parsley, to garnish

1 Beat together the eggs and egg yolks. Season with salt and nutmeg. Bring the milk to a boil, then remove from the heat. Pour the egg mixture into the milk, stirring constantly. Strain through a fine-mesh sieve. Season again to taste with salt and nutmeg.

2 Butter a 4 × 4in (10 × 10cm) baking pan. Pour the egg mixture into the pan and cover it. Place the baking pan over a pan of simmering water. Cook the egg mixture for 15 minutes, or until it has set. Let cool slightly, then refrigerate for 1 hour, until the custard has cooled completely. Cut into ½in (1cm) cubes.

3 Heat the stock. In a second saucepan, bring salted water to a boil. Meanwhile, peel the asparagus spears and cut them into ½in (1cm) pieces. Blanch the asparagus and cauliflower florets in boiling water for 8 minutes. Remove from the water and divide the vegetables and egg custard among the soup bowls. Ladle hot beef stock over the cauliflower and custard. Sprinkle with parsley and serve immediately.

ROSIN'S TIP: The broth from the boiled beef on page 80 makes great beef stock. For a heartier soup, add mini meatballs made from the ground meat mixture used in the Königsberg veal dumplings (see page 96).

SCALLION SOUP WITH POTATO AND BACON DUMPLINGS

Foam doesn't just make the soup look frothy—it also produces a more interesting texture and gives the soup a glossy appearance.

> **serves 4**
> **1 hour**

1 To make the dumplings, boil the potatoes in salted water for 20 minutes, until tender. Remove from the heat, then drain and peel them.

2 Meanwhile, cut the bread into small cubes. Dice the bacon. Peel and chop the shallot. Finely chop the chervil. Heat the butter in a frying pan, add the bread cubes, and fry until golden brown. Remove and set aside. Add the oil, bacon, and shallots to the pan, and sauté.

3 Place a saucepan of salted water over low heat. Mash the still-warm potatoes in a bowl, add the bread, bacon, onions, and egg, and combine well. Season to taste with salt, pepper, and chervil. Using a teaspoon, form 16 small dumplings from the potato mixture. Roll each between the palms of your hands and place the dumplings in barely simmering salted water. Poach for 5 minutes. Remove from the water and set aside.

4 For the soup, peel and dice the shallot. Finely chop the white part of the scallions. Cut the scallion greens into 4 strips. Heat 1 tablespoon of the butter in a saucepan. Add the shallots and sauté until translucent. Season with salt, pepper, and sugar. Sauté for 1 minute more and deglaze with the wine. Reduce the liquid by half.

5 Add the stock, scallions, and crème fraîche to the soup. Simmer for 5 minutes, then remove from the heat. Blend the soup with a handheld blender. Season to taste with salt, pepper, and sugar. Add the remaining cold butter, and immediately mount the butter (see below) with a handheld blender until the soup is foamy. Ladle the soup into heatproof glass jars. Thread the potato-and-bacon dumplings and strips of scallion onto wooden skewers and balance them over the mouth of the jars. Serve immediately.

DUMPLINGS
7oz (200g) Russet Burbank potatoes
salt
1 slice white bread
1½oz (40g) smoked bacon
½ shallot
1 small bunch of chervil leaves
1 tbsp unsalted butter
1 tbsp canola oil
1 egg
freshly ground black pepper

SOUP
1 shallot
2 bunches of scallions
2 tbsp cold unsalted butter
salt and freshly ground black pepper
sugar
½ cup white wine
5 cups vegetable stock
2 tbsp crème fraîche

 ROSIN'S TIP: In cooking, "mounting" is the term used to describe the process of making a foam. To do this, chilled butter is mixed into the soup, creating a perfect foam that won't collapse.

FOAMED **GARLIC** **SOUP** WITH WHITE WINE

Wild garlic is in season in March and April. Made from the leaves, this quick and easy soup has a refreshing taste. If you can't find wild garlic, or if you would like to vary this recipe, substitute mixed spring herbs, such as parsley, chervil, chives, dill, and tarragon.

> serves 4
> 40 minutes

2 shallots
6 tbsp unsalted butter, chilled
    and cubed
sugar
salt
1 large bunch of wild garlic,
    about 5½oz (150g)
⅔ cup white wine
2½ cups vegetable stock
¾ cup heavy cream

1 Peel and dice the shallots. Melt 4 tablespoons of the butter in a saucepan. Add the shallots and sauté until translucent. Season with sugar and salt. Finely chop 2 wild garlic leaves and set aside. Place the remaining leaves in the saucepan. Deglaze with the wine. Let boil for a few minutes, then add the stock. Simmer for 5 minutes.

2 Remove the soup from the heat. Purée the soup using a handheld blender. Strain the liquid through a sieve set over a saucepan. Reheat the soup, stir in the cream, and simmer for 5 minutes.

3 Remove the soup from the heat. Season again to taste with salt and sugar. Add the remaining butter. Using a handheld blender, blend until foamy. Ladle the soup into bowls. Sprinkle with the reserved wild garlic. Serve immediately.

ROSIN'S TIP: The narrow wild garlic leaves look very similar to poisonous lily of the valley leaves, so don't gather them from the wild yourself. Plant your own wild garlic or buy it at a farmers' market.

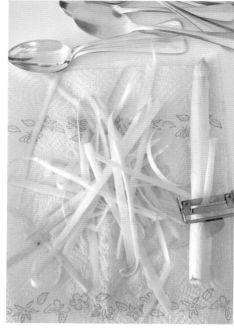

FOAMED ASPARAGUS SOUP WITH WHITE WINE

I admit, this recipe sounds extraordinarily simple. And it is. The soup becomes so richly flavored and delicious because of the time spent cooking it—time is the best ingredient. We season through cooking, not through seasoning. Reducing the stock gives the soup strength and flavor.

> serves 4
> 45 minutes

1 Place the stock, white wine, and asparagus in a saucepan. Bring to a boil. Simmer for 30 minutes. Strain through a sieve into a second saucepan. Discard the asparagus and trimmings. Reduce the liquid by a third.

2 Remove the saucepan from the heat. Add the butter and crème fraîche and beat the soup until foamy. Season to taste with salt, pepper, sugar, nutmeg, and lemon juice. Serve immediately in small glass jars.

1¼ cups vegetable stock
¾ cup white wine
1 bunch of white asparagus pieces, or trimmings
4 tbsp cold unsalted butter
⅔ cup crème fraîche
salt
freshly ground black pepper
sugar
freshly grated nutmeg
lemon juice

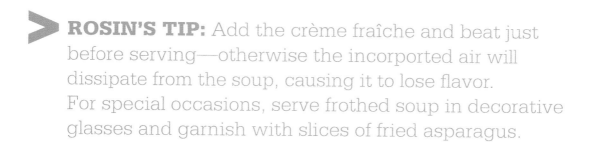

ROSIN'S TIP: Add the crème fraîche and beat just before serving—otherwise the incorported air will dissipate from the soup, causing it to lose flavor.
For special occasions, serve frothed soup in decorative glasses and garnish with slices of fried asparagus.

CHILLED VEGETABLE SOUP
WITH CHILI CROUTONS

I became familiar with this light, refreshing soup in Spain when I was young. We always stayed in Spain with friends, and the father of the family made it for us. Feta cheese, crumbled into small pieces and scattered over the soup, makes a delicious addition.

> serves 4–6
> 30 minutes + 1 hour to bake

4 slices of white bread
1 large red chili pepper
1¼ cups olive oil
juice of 1 lemon
2 shallots
1 garlic clove
4 vine tomatoes
2 yellow bell peppers
1 English cucumber
3 celery stalks
1½ cups ice cubes
½ bunch of cilantro
salt
freshly ground black pepper
Tabasco sauce

1 Preheat the oven to 225°F (110°C). Cut the bread into ¾in (2cm) cubes and arrange them on a baking sheet. Place the sheet on the center rack and let the bread cubes dry for 1 hour. Cut a slice off the bottom of the chili pepper, and chop it finely. Combine with ½ cup of olive oil and 2 squeezes of lemon juice. Just before serving, remove the bread from the oven. Place the bread cubes in a bowl and drizzle with the chili oil.

2 Peel and dice the shallots and garlic clove. Heat 1 tablespoon of olive oil in the frying pan. Add the shallots and garlic and sauté until translucent.

Remove the seeds from the tomatoes, bell peppers, cucumbers, and the remainder of the chili pepper. Chop the vegetables coarsely. Cut the celery stalks into ½in (1cm) pieces. Using a blender, or handheld blender, purée the raw vegetables and the sautéed shallots and garlic.

3 Add the remaining lemon juice, ice cubes, cilantro, and the remaining olive oil. Blend everything on the highest setting for 2 minutes. Season to taste with salt, pepper, and Tabasco sauce. Serve immediately with the croutons.

ROSIN'S TIP: Puréeing changes the consistency of soups and sauces, making them thicker and creamier. It also deepens the flavors of fruits and vegetables. Lightly puréed vegetable soups are more pleasing to the palate than chunky soups.

POTATO SOUP
WITH SMOKED BACON

In the German army, potato soup was served on long marches. By the time the break came, we were all famished, and the potato soup served from the field kitchen tasted amazing. I also cooked in the German army, so this recipe is the real deal.

> **serves 6**
> **30 minutes**

1 Peel the potatoes and cut them into ¾in (2cm) pieces. Peel and dice the onion. Slice the leek into thin strips. Dice the bacon. Place the butter in a deep saucepan, add the bacon, and fry. Add the onion and leek and sauté. Deglaze with the white wine. Add the potatoes and bay leaves. Pour in the vegetable stock.

2 Bring the soup to a boil, then boil until the potatoes are tender. Using a handheld blender, purée the soup. Don't purée it too finely—pieces of potato should be visible. Return the soup to a boil. Season to taste with salt, pepper, and nutmeg. Divide among bowls. Place a dollop of fresh cheese on top. Sprinkle with parsley and serve.

1lb 5oz (600g) Russet Burbank potatoes
1 onion
½ leek, just the white part
2oz (60g) smoked bacon
3 tbsp unsalted butter
½ cup white wine
2 bay leaves
6 cups vegetable stock
salt and freshly ground black pepper
freshly grated nutmeg
3 tbsp fresh cheese, such as quark or ricotta, or sour cream
1 tbsp chopped parsley, to garnish

ROSIN'S TIP: For meat-lovers, add meatballs or smoked sausage as well as bacon. To transform this recipe into a delicious summer soup, make it with sweet potatoes and finish with a dash of Tabasco and a pinch of curry powder.

MICRO-GREEN SOUP
WITH CRÈME FRAÎCHE

Micro-greens have been popular in fine restaurants for a number of years now.
They're good food—nutrient-rich and packed with flavor.

> serves 4
> 30 minutes

1 medium potato
1 shallot
1 garlic clove
4 tbsp cold, unsalted butter
salt
sugar
⅔ cup white wine
2 cups vegetable stock
¾ cup crème fraîche
2 large bunches of mixed
   micro-greens
freshly ground black pepper
lemon juice

1 Peel the potato and cut it into ½in (1cm) cubes. Peel and dice the shallot and garlic cloves. Melt half of the butter in a saucepan. Add the shallot and garlic and sauté until translucent. Season to taste with salt and sugar. Deglaze with white wine. Reduce the liquid by half. Add the potato. Pour in the stock and simmer for 10 minutes.

2 Add the crème fraîche. Return the soup to a boil and remove it from the heat. Add the micro-greens and the remaining butter. Using a handheld blender, blend the soup until foamy. Season to taste with salt, sugar, pepper, and lemon juice. Ladle the soup into bowls and serve immediately.

ROSIN'S TIP: Frothing soups is not just a fashion trend—the air introduced during frothing binds the soup and gives it a lovely consistency. When tasting for seasoning before you froth, remember that the added air reduces the intensity of the flavor.

TOMATO AND BASIL SOUP
WITH VEGETABLES

In the 1970s my mother took a cooking course and brought home a recipe for tomato soup that was a big family favorite. Today, I can't decide whether I prefer clear or bound tomato soup—I love them both. Here is a recipe for bound tomato soup.

> serves 4–6
> 25 minutes + 1 hour to cook

1 Peel and dice the shallots, garlic, carrot, and celery root. Dice the leek. Heat the olive oil in a saucepan and add the prepared vegetables. Sweat the vegetables over low heat. Stir in the tomato paste and cook for 1 minute more. Add the peeled tomatoes and white wine. Pour in the vegetable stock. Add the bay leaves, clove, and sprig of thyme. Season with salt, pepper, and sugar. Bring to a boil and simmer gently for 1 hour.

2 Gently tear the basil leaves. Remove the saucepan from the heat. Using a slotted spoon, remove the thyme, clove, and bay leaves from the soup. Purée the soup with a handheld blender. Season to taste with salt, pepper, and sugar. Ladle the soup into bowls. Sprinkle with the basil. Serve immediately.

4 shallots
1 garlic clove
1 carrot
¼ head of celery root
½ leek
2 tbsp olive oil
2 tbsp tomato paste
3lb (1¼kg) peeled, canned tomatoes
1¼ cups white wine
4 cups vegetable stock
2 bay leaves
1 clove
1 sprig of thyme
salt
freshly ground black pepper
sugar
2 bunchs of basil leaves, to garnish

ROSIN'S TIP: Don't feel guilty about using canned tomatoes in this recipe— they will produce a soup with a rich, robust tomato flavor.

TOMATO ESSENCE
WITH BOUQUET GARNI

Serve this lovely tea between courses when you are serving a full-course menu.
It's refreshing and spectacularly eye-catching.

> serves 6
> 2 hours

6 garlic cloves
5½lb (2½kg) peeled, canned
   tomatoes
10½ cups vegetable stock
¼ cup sugar
2 sprigs of rosemary
2 sprigs of thyme
1 bunch of basil leaves
6 garlic cloves
8 bay leaves
10 peppercorns
2 cups egg whites
1–1½ cups of ice cubes
1 bunch of rosemary leaves
1 bunch of thyme leaves

1 Peel and chop the garlic. Place the garlic, tomatoes, stock, sugar, herbs, and spices in a saucepan. Bring to a boil over medium heat.

2 Strain the liquid through a sieve into a second saucepan, pressing lightly on the tomatoes. In a bowl, beat the egg whites until foamy, but not stiff. Stir in the ice cubes. Add the egg whites to the liquid. Place the saucepan on the stove and bring the liquid to a boil over medium heat.

3 With a slotted spoon, skim the surface of the liquid and discard the scum. Slowly stir the egg whites so they don't stick to the bottom of the saucepan. Remove the saucepan from the heat once the liquid begins to boil. Strain the liquid through a sieve lined with paper towels into a second saucepan. Return the liquid to a boil and reduce to 6 cups.

4 Chop the rosemary and thyme. Remove the contents from 4 teabags and fill them with the rosemary and thyme. Tie with kitchen twine. Place 1 bouquet garni in each teacup and pour in the hot tomato essence. Steep for 4 minutes. Serve immediately.

ROSIN'S TIP: Season the tomato essense with herbs to create flavors that match different menus. The technique of using egg whites to purify stock works with all clear broths.

MEAT
AND POULTRY

PERFECT **BEEF FILLET**

Professional chefs and home cooks alike often ask what's the best way to cook the perfect beef fillet. This recipe answers that question. The pan must be very hot, or the juices will escape from the meat and it will poach rather than fry. The meat should, however, cook slowly in the oven.

> serves 4
> 25 minutes

4 beef fillets, about
   7oz (200g) each
freshly ground black pepper
herb salt (see page 219)
1 tbsp olive oil
5 garlic cloves
1 tbsp unsalted butter
2 sprigs of rosemary

1 Preheat a convection oven to 225°F (100°C) or a conventional oven to 250°F (115°C). Season the beef to taste with pepper and herb salt. Heat a frying pan and add the olive oil. Sear the fillets on each side for 1 minute over high heat, until the meat is browned. Remove from the frying pan and place the fillets on a baking sheet.

2 Using the blade of a knife, flatten the garlic cloves. Melt the butter in the frying pan. Add the rosemary and garlic and gently shake them in the pan. Distribute them over the fillets. Place the baking sheet on the center rack of the oven and cook the fillets for 10 minutes. Remove from the oven. Let rest for 5 minutes before serving.

ROSIN'S TIP: Serve the fillet with sautéed new potatoes. Place 12 new potatoes in a saucepan of salted water and add ½ garlic clove and 2 sprigs of rosemary. Bring to a boil, cook for 10–15 minutes, and drain. Cut the potatoes in half. Heat 2 tablespoons of olive oil in a frying pan. Place them, cut-side down, in the pan and fry until crisp. Drain the oil. Add salt, ½ cup of tomato salsa (see page 218), and chopped rosemary. Serve immediately.

ROSIN FAMILY
SAUERBRATEN

This is the traditional Rosin family Christmas dinner. We serve the sauerbraten with dumplings and pear preserves on the side. Marinate the meat for the full three days—the acidity in the marinade tenderizes the meat beautifully.

> serves 6
> 1½ hours + 3 days to marinate + 3 hours to braise

1 Peel and dice the carrots and celery root. Dice the leek. Place the vegetables, bay leaves, cloves, red wine, red wine vinegar, salt, peppercorns, and juniper berries in a large saucepan. Bring to a boil. Remove from the heat, then pour the marinade over the beef. Cover the meat and refrigerate for 3 days.

2 Remove the meat, then strain the marinade. Reserve the vegetables and spices in one bowl and the liquid in another. Heat 3 tablespoons of oil in a Dutch oven. Add the beef. Sear it on all sides over high heat, then remove from the Dutch oven. Add the reserved vegetables and spices and fry until browned. Stir in the tomato paste. Fry for 2 minutes. Deglaze with half the marinade and the beef stock. Add the beef to the pot. Bring to a boil. Reduce the heat and simmer for 2–3 hours. Add more marinade, as needed.

3 Just before the beef is cooked, peel and dice the shallots. Heat 1 tablespoon of canola oil in a frying pan. Add the shallots and sauté until translucent. Sprinkle with sugar. Stir the sugar until it caramelizes. Deglaze with Port wine and boil vigorously.

4 Remove the pot roast from the braising liquid. Let the meat cool and carve it into slices. Strain the braising liquid through a sieve and add it to the Port wine reduction. Reduce the liquid to 2 cups.

5 Just before serving, beat the chilled butter a little at time into the braising liquid to bind the sauce. Season again to taste with salt and sugar. Place the slices of beef in the sauce to warm. Divide the meat among the plates. Serve immediately.

2 carrots
½ head of celery root
2 leeks
4 bay leaves
3 cloves
6 cups red wine
6 cups red wine vinegar
1 tbsp salt
10 peppercorns
8 juniper berries
2lb 4oz (1kg) boneless beef shank or rump roast
¼ cup canola oil
2 tbsp tomato paste
3 cups beef stock
4 shallots
¼ cup sugar
3 cups red Port wine
6 tbsp cold, unsalted butter, cut into pieces

 ROSIN'S TIP: Marinating meat tenderizes it and enriches the flavor of the sauce. Cover the marinade in plastic wrap or store it in an airtight container so the flavor isn't absorbed by other foods in the fridge.

ROAST BEEF
WITH HORSERADISH AND APPLE

When simmered gently in beef stock, roast beef becomes very flavorful. The concentrated broth it produces is an added bonus—it's great in savory soups and sauces.

> **serves 6–8**
> **1 hour + 3 hours to cook**

5 quarts (5 liters) beef stock
4lb 8oz (2kg) boneless round of beef or eye of round roast
2 bay leaves
2 cloves
5 allspice berries
10 peppercorns
2 carrots
½ head of celery root
1 onion
1 garlic clove
½ leek
1 handful of chervil leaves
1 shallot
½ fresh horseradish root
1 apple
1 tbsp unsalted butter
1 cup crème fraîche
salt
freshly ground black pepper

1 Place the beef stock in a large saucepan and heat it to 200°F (90°C). Place the roast beef in the stock. Add the bay leaves, cloves, allspice, and peppercorns. Let the meat simmer gently for 1½ hours.

2 Peel and dice the carrots, celery root, onion, and garlic. Slice the leek. Place the vegetables and chervil in the saucepan and simmer gently for 1½ hours. Remove the meat from the pan and let it rest for 15 minutes. Carve into ½in (1cm) slices before serving.

3 Peel and dice the shallot. Peel the horseradish. Cut the apple in half and remove the core. Melt the butter in a frying pan. Add the shallots and sauté until translucent. Add a bit of the beef broth to the shallots. Stir in the crème fraîche. Simmer for 5 minutes. Remove the pan from the heat and season the sauce to taste with salt and pepper. Purée with a handheld blender until foamy. Arrange the slices of roast beef on the plates. Grate the horseradish and apple over the meat. Spoon the sauce over the beef. Serve.

ROSIN'S TIP:
Strain the stock through
a sieve and serve it, along
with a few vegetables,
as an appetizer. If the flavor
of the broth is too strong,
thin it with a little water.

PAN-FRIED VEAL
IN WHITE WINE SAUCE

When I was training to become a chef in the 1980s, it seemed like we made this dish by the bucketful. Zurich-style fried veal with rösti was the epitome of good bourgeois cuisine. Today, this dish isn't seen on menus very often, which I think is a real shame.

> **serves 4**
> **25 minutes**

1 Cut the veal into strips ½in (1cm) wide and ¼in (5mm) thick. Season to taste with salt and pepper. Peel and dice the shallot. Finely chop the mushrooms.

2 Heat the oil in a frying pan. Add the veal, and fry until browned and just cooked. Remove from the pan. Place the mushrooms in the frying pan, and sauté them. Add the shallots and sauté a few minutes more. Deglaze with white wine and add the veal juices. Reduce the sauce for 5 minutes, until thick and creamy.

3 Stir in the cheese. Season to taste with salt and pepper. Return the veal to the sauce to warm. Divide the veal among the plates and sprinkle with parsley. Serve immediately.

1lb 2oz (500g) boneless veal loin
salt
freshly ground black pepper
1 shallot
14oz (400g) button or cremini mushrooms
2 tbsp canola oil
⅔ cup white wine
½ cup gravy (from the goulash [see page 84] or the beef cheeks [see page 91])
1 cup fresh cheese, such as quark, or sour cream
1 tsp chopped parsley, to garnish

 ROSIN'S TIP: The gravy is the secret to the richness of the sauce. Rösti is usually served with this dish, although potato pancakes (see page 163) are also a good pairing.

GOULASH WITH BELL PEPPERS AND TOMATOES

We had goulash at home almost weekly when I was growing up, and my mother always made a cucumber salad to go with it. Today, I know that the acidity of the cucumber salad marries beautifully with the goulash, so I recommend serving it with this dish.

> serves 4–6
> 2 hours + 1½ hours to braise

12 shallots
4 tbsp olive oil
1lb 10oz (750g) boneless pork shoulder
1lb 10oz (750g) chuck roast
2 tbsp tomato paste
2 cups red wine
3 cups vegetable or beef stock
2 bay leaves
2 cloves
salt
freshly ground black pepper
medium-hot Hungarian paprika
2 tbsp cornstarch
2 red bell peppers
5 medium tomatoes
sugar

1 Peel and slice the shallots. Heat 3 tablespoons of olive oil in a large saucepan. Add the meat and sear over high heat. Reduce the heat to medium, add the shallots and sauté for 10–15 minutes. Don't worry if the meat sticks to the bottom of the pan, since it will come off during deglazing.

2 Stir in the tomato paste. Deglaze with the red wine, then the stock. Keep stirring until the bottom of the saucepan has been scraped clean and the meat residue has dissolved. Add the bay leaves and cloves. Season to taste with salt, pepper, and paprika. Simmer for 1½ hours, or until the meat is tender.

3 Strain the goulash through a sieve placed over a saucepan. In a bowl, stir a little water into the cornstarch, then add it to the saucepan. Return the sauce to a boil. Reduce until the flavor is rich and full. Add the meat to the sauce.

4 Peel the bell peppers, remove the seeds and pith, and cut them into ¾in (2cm) cubes. Blanch the tomatoes in boiling water. Remove the skins, cut them into quarters, and remove the seeds. Before serving, heat the remaining olive oil in a frying pan. Add the bell peppers and sauté for 3 minutes before adding the tomatoes. Season with salt and sugar and remove the pan from the stove. Divide the goulash among the plates. Top with the tomatoes and peppers. Serve.

ROSIN'S TIP: The cut of meat makes a big difference to the quality of the dish, so always consult your butcher when buying meat. Freeze leftover sauce and use it with cod (see page 126) or pan-fried veal (see page 83).

BRAISED **BEEF CHEEKS** IN WINE SAUCE

I can't count how many times we've served this dish in the restaurant or at catered events. It is the perfect marriage of hearty fare and delicate flavors. If I may say so, it is absolutely scrumptious, especially the sauce. No other cut of meat yields such a deeply flavored sauce as beef cheeks. It's wonderful with mashed potatoes (see page 159).

> serves 4
> 45 minutes + 3 hours to cook

1 Peel and coarsely chop the carrots and celery root. Cut the leek into slices. Heat the oil in a Dutch oven. Place the beef cheeks in the saucepan and sear it on all sides over high heat. Add the tomato paste and chopped vegetables and fry with the beef cheeks for 5 minutes. Pour in the red wine and Port wine. Stir well, scraping the bottom of the saucepan to release any meat stuck on the bottom. Pour in the beef stock. Bring to a boil and simmer over low heat for 3 hours, until the beef cheeks are tender.

2 Remove the beef cheeks from the saucepan and set them aside. Pour the cooking liquid through a sieve into a saucepan. Add the rosemary and bay leaves. Return to a boil and reduce the sauce until it has a lovely consistency. This will take about 20 minutes. Strain the sauce through a sieve. Season it with salt and sugar. Keep warm.

3 Just before serving, remove any fat from the cooled beef cheeks and slice them into 4 portions. Warm the meat in the sauce. Serve immediately.

1 carrot
½ head of celery root
1 leek
5 tbsp canola oil
2 beef cheeks with fat layer, about 2lb 4oz (1kg) each
⅓ tomato paste
4 cups red wine
4 cups Port wine
8½ cups beef stock
1 sprig of rosemary
2 bay leaves
salt
sugar

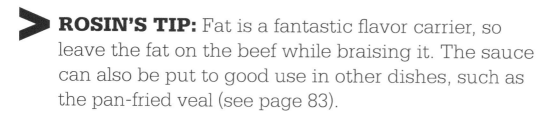

ROSIN'S TIP: Fat is a fantastic flavor carrier, so leave the fat on the beef while braising it. The sauce can also be put to good use in other dishes, such as the pan-fried veal (see page 83).

LEG OF RABBIT
WITH POTATOES AND BELL PEPPERS

Rabbit should always be cooked gently, so that it remains juicy and flavorful. In this recipe, Hungarian paprika salami and capers give the meat an extra spiciness.

> serves 4
> 40 minutes + 40 minutes to braise

4 rabbit legs
sea salt
Hungarian paprika
14oz (400g) Yukon Gold
   potatoes
4 red bell peppers
6 shallots
4oz (120g) Hungarian paprika
   salami or any Spanish-style
   chorizo
½ cup olive oil
⅔ cup white wine
2 cups chicken stock
½ bunch of basil
12 caper berries
freshly ground black pepper

1 Rub the rabbit legs with the sea salt and paprika. Peel the potatoes and cut them into pieces. Peel the red bell peppers, remove the seeds and pith, and cut them into strips. Peel and chop the shallots. Dice the salami. Preheat a convection oven to 325°F (160°C) or a conventional oven to 350°F (175°C).

2 Heat 2 tablespoons of olive oil in a roasting pan. Sear the rabbit legs for 7 minutes, turning halfway through. Remove from the pan. Put the potatoes, bell peppers, shallots, and salami in the pan. Sauté for 10 minutes, until browned.

3 Return the rabbit legs to the saucepan. Deglaze with white wine and stock. Add the basil and caper berries and stir to combine. Bring to a boil and remove from the heat. Place the roasting pan on the center rack of the oven and bake for 40 minutes.

4 Remove the roasting pan from the oven and divide the vegetables among the plates. Drizzle them with the remaining olive oil and season to taste with salt and pepper. Arrange the rabbit legs with the vegetables. Serve immediately.

ROSIN'S TIP: Until the 1960s, rabbit was commonly served in Germany. With the resurgance of light cuisine, this tender white meat is returning to our menus. Rabbit is less fatty than chicken and turkey and has a higher mineral content.

EASTERN EUROPEAN SAUERKRAUT STEW

East European influences have had a big impact on German cooking, and not just over the past 70 years. My ancestors were from East Prussia, and stews such as this one, known in Poland as "bigos," have played a large role in our family's cooking.

> serves 4–6
> 30 minutes + 1 hour to cook

1 Dice the bacon. Peel and chop the onions and garlic. Heat 1 tablespoon of the oil in a saucepan. Add the bacon, onions, and garlic and sauté until the bacon is crisp. Add the sauerkraut and sauté for 5 minutes more.

2 Add the tomato paste. Pour in 3¼ cups of vegetable stock and stir. Add the peppercorns, bay leaves, and marjoram. Bring to a boil and partially cover the saucepan. Simmer for 1 hour, stirring reguarly, until the sauerkraut is cooked. Add stock as needed.

3 Clean the mushrooms and cut them into quarters. Heat the remaining oil in a frying pan. Add the mushrooms and sauté until golden brown. Season to taste with salt and pepper. Stir the mushrooms into the sauerkraut. Season with salt and pepper, divide among the plates, and serve.

VEGETARIAN STEW: Omit the bacon and double the quantity of mushrooms to 14oz (400g). For a smoky flavor, season the stew with smoked salt and Pimentón de la Vera.

14oz (400g) smoked bacon
2 onions
1 garlic clove
2 tbsp canola oil
2lb 10oz (1.2kg) sauerkraut
¼ cup tomato paste
4 cups vegetable stock
10 peppercorns
4 bay leaves
1 tsp dried marjoram
7oz (200g) brown mushrooms
salt
freshly ground black pepper

 ROSIN'S TIP: Smoked sausage also works well in this stew. If you like, top the stew with a dollop of sour cream or crème fraîche.

KÖNIGSBERG VEAL DUMPLINGS
IN CAPER SAUCE

This is one of my favorite dishes, and I like it best when it's served in a bowl with a large serving of sauce. Don't make the dumplings too big—less is more in this case.

> serves 4–6
> 2 hours

2 day-old bread rolls
½ cup milk
3 shallots
6 tbsp capers
2 tbsp canola oil
2lb 4oz (1kg) ground veal
2 large eggs
2 tbsp mustard
salt
freshly ground black pepper
1 onion
1 bay leaf
1 clove
2 tbsp potato starch
⅓ cup white wine vinegar
sugar

1 Chop the bread rolls coarsely and soak them in the milk for 20 minutes. Peel and dice the shallots. Chop the capers. Heat 2 tablespoons of the oil in a frying pan. Add the shallots, and sauté until translucent. Place them in a bowl. Squeeze the bread to remove the milk. Add the bread, veal, eggs, mustard, 4 tablespoons of the capers, salt, and pepper to the bowl. Combine well.

2 Heat 8½ cups of salted water in a saucepan. Stud the onion with the bay leaf and clove. Add a little caper water (from the jar) to the saucepan. Use a tablespoon to scoop up pieces of the ground meat mixture. Moisten your hands and shape small dumplings from the ground meat. Place the dumplings in the simmering water. Remove with a slotted spoon as soon as they float to the surface. Set aside.

3 Reduce the cooking water by two-thirds. In a small bowl, mix the potato starch with cold water and add it to the reduced stock to thicken it. Add the remaining capers and the vinegar. Season the sauce with salt, pepper, and sugar. Place the veal dumplings in the sauce to warm them. Divide the meatballs among bowls. Blend the sauce with a handheld blender and pour a generous amount over the dumplings. Serve immediately.

ROSIN'S TIP: Buttered potatoes go perfectly with this dish. Cook unpeeled potatoes until tender, cool them slightly before peeling them, then toss them in butter.

CURRY WURST IN FRUIT SAUCE

Curry wurst is a staple of Ruhr food culture and is found on the menu of every French-fry stand there. This sauce contains no artificial ingredients, which makes it great for those who want fresh food.

> serves 4
> 40 minutes

1 Peel and dice the shallot and garlic. Remove the seeds from the chili pepper and chop it finely. Remove the stems and seeds from the bell peppers and coarsely chop the bell peppers.

2 Heat the oil in a frying pan. Add the shallot and garlic and sauté until translucent. Add all the peppers and fry until the liquid has evaporated. Stir in the sugar, tomato paste, chili, and vanilla seeds, and sauté . Pour in the stock. Simmer until the sauce is creamy.

3 Meanwhile, grill the sausages on the barbeque or under the broiler until they are crisp on the outside and fully cooked. Remove the saucepan from the heat. Purée the sauce with a handheld blender until smooth. Season to taste with salt, curry powder, and paprika. Place the sausages in paper or plastic containers and cover with sauce. Serve immediately.

1 shallot
1 garlic clove
½ red chili pepper
4 red bell peppers
1 tbsp canola oil
1 heaped tbsp sugar
2 tbsp tomato paste
seeds of ½ vanilla bean
1¾ cups vegetable stock
4 white sausages, such as
   bratwurst, about 3½oz
   (100g) each
salt
hot curry powder
paprika

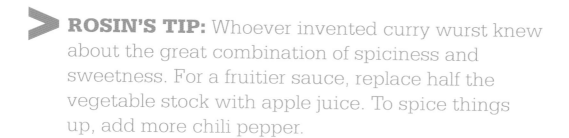

> **ROSIN'S TIP:** Whoever invented curry wurst knew about the great combination of spiciness and sweetness. For a fruitier sauce, replace half the vegetable stock with apple juice. To spice things up, add more chili pepper.

ROAST BEEF WITH EGGPLANT CAVIAR AND TOMATO SALSA

So easy to prepare, this eggplant caviar brings forth the richness and unique flavor of the eggplant. Don't purée the eggplant until it's smooth—leave it a bit chunky. As the great chef Eckart Witzigmann said to me: "Little pieces, Boy, little pieces!"

> serves 6–8
> 35 minutes

4 medium eggplants
1 sprig of rosemary
1 lime
1 garlic clove
1 tbsp parsley leaves
olive oil
salt
freshly ground black pepper
10½oz (300g) rare roast beef,
    fat trimmed

TOMATO SALSA
see page 218

1 Preheat the oven to 350°F (180°C). Remove the stems from the eggplants and place the eggplants on a baking sheet with the rosemary sprig. Put the baking sheet on the center rack of the oven. Bake for 15–20 minutes, until the peels burst open. Squeeze the lime. Peel the garlic.

2 Remove the eggplant from the oven and peel them. Using a handheld blender, purée the eggplant together with the garlic, parsley, and lime juice to make a chunky paste. Season to taste with olive oil, salt, and pepper.

3 Cut the beef into thin slices and fan them out on plates. Scatter tomato salsa over the top and let the meat rest for a few moments. Top the roast beef with several dollops of eggplant caviar. Serve immediately.

ROSIN'S TIP: I recommend using Tasmanian black pepper. It's pricey, but sensationally flavorful. Eggplant caviar served on toasted bread makes a great appetizer. Top the eggplant with salsa and lemon zest, then season with freshly ground pepper.

PORK BELLY
WITH CRACKLING

Young pork belly is one of my new favorite dishes. Gently cooking the meat in heat-resistant plastic wrap not only makes it taste especially good, but also produces a tender meat that melts in your mouth like butter. This is home cooking, sous-vide (see below) style.

> **serves 4–6**
> **15 minutes + 14 hours to cook**

1 Preheat a convection oven to 175°F (80°C) or a regular oven to 200°F (95°C). Peel and chop the garlic. Place the pork belly in a casserole dish. Distribute the remaining ingredients evenly over the skin. Wrap the casserole dish with heat-resistant plastic wrap so that it is airtight. Place the dish in the oven and bake it slowly for at least 14 hours.

2 Take the casserole dish out of the oven and let the pork belly cool. Remove the pork from the casserole dish. Scrape the spices off the skin. Cut the pork belly into quarters. Heat a frying pan and place the pieces of pork belly, skin-side down, in the pan. Fry slowly over low heat for 20 minutes, until the skin becomes crisp. Serve immediately.

3 garlic cloves
1lb 12oz (800g) boneless suckling pork belly, skin on
2 sprigs of thyme
2 tsp sea salt
freshly ground black pepper
6 tbsp canola oil

ROSIN'S TIP: Sous-vide is a French term that means "vacuum sealed." Meat, fish, or vegetables are placed in a vacuum-sealed bag and cooked in water or steam at low heat. In a steam cooker set to 175°F (80°C), the pork belly cooks in 8 hours.

BEEF ROULADES
IN BACON AND
RED WINE SAUCE

At my mother's house, beef roulades were always a big favorite, and somehow hers always turned out perfectly. When I asked what the secret was, she answered: "You have to put a lot of tastiness in them." So, here's a recipe full of tastiness.

> **serves 4**
> **1½ hours + 2 hours to cook**

4 thin slices of flank steak,
    about 5½oz (150g) each
2 shallots
4 dill pickles (optional)
1 carrot
1 onion
¼ head of celery root
4 slices of bacon
4 tsp mustard
3 tbsp tomato paste
4 tbsp canola oil
salt
freshly ground black pepper
sugar
2 bay leaves
2 cloves
10 peppercorns
2 sprigs of rosemary
6 cups red wine
2 cups beef stock

1 Place the steaks between plastic wrap and pound until thin. Peel and slice the shallots into rings. Slice the pickles, if using. Peel and chop the carrots, onion, and celery root. Cut the bacon into strips. Combine the mustard and 1 tablespoon of tomato paste in a bowl.

2 Heat 1 tablespoon of oil in a frying pan. Add the shallots and sauté until translucent. Season to taste with salt, pepper, and sugar. Sauté until the sugar caramelizes. Remove from the pan. Add 1 tablespoon of oil to the pan, add the bacon, and cook until crisp. Remove the frying pan from the heat.

3 Arrange the steaks on a work surface. Season to taste with salt and pepper. Spread with the mustard and tomato paste mixture. Top evenly with the shallots and bacon. Place pickle slices on top. Roll the roulades tightly and secure with toothpicks. Heat the remaining oil in a deep saucepan.

4 Sear the roulades evenly over high heat. Remove from the pan. Place the carrot, onion, and celery root in the saucepan and sauté. Season with salt and sugar. Stir in the remaining tomato paste. Add the bay leaves, cloves, peppercorns, and rosemary, and cook for 2 minutes. Deglaze with the red wine and stock. Bring to a boil and season to taste again. Return the roulades to the pan, cover, and simmer for 2 hours.

5 Remove the roulades from the saucepan. Strain the sauce through a sieve and return it to the saucepan. Boil for 1 hour, until the sauce is thick and creamy. Season with sugar and freshly ground black pepper. Return the roulades to the sauce to warm. Divide them the among the plates, top with gravy, and serve.

ROSIN'S TIP: For extra flavor, add 1 tablespoon of mustard to the sauce. Do this at the very end, because mustard loses its flavor when heated.

GUINEA HEN WITH CELERY ROOT SALAD

I'm known for not letting food go to waste. Using up leftovers is an art, plus it makes good economic sense. With this recipe, leftover bread dumplings are put to use in a new and surprising way.

> serves 4
> 40 minutes + 8 hours to dry + 1 hour to marinate

1 Preheat the oven to 200°F (90°C). Chop the dumplings and arrange them on a baking sheet. Put the baking sheet on the center rack of the oven and dry the dumplings for 8 hours.

2 For the salad, peel the celery root and cut it into ¼in (5mm) cubes. Blanch for 4 minutes in boiling salted water. Plunge into ice-cold water to cool, then drain. In a bowl, whisk the olive oil and lemon juice together. Add the celery root and toss. Season with salt and pepper. Marinate for at least 1 hour.

3 To make the guinea hen breasts, crumble the bread dumplings and place them on a plate. Season the guinea hen with salt and freshly ground black pepper. Press both sides of the breasts into the crumbs until they are evenly covered. Heat the butter in a frying pan. Fry the breasts over medium heat for 6 minutes on each side.

4 Divide the celery root salad among the plates and crumble the Feta cheese over the top. Serve with micro-greens and the crispy breasts of guinea hen.

4 bread dumplings
   (see page 164)
1 head of celery root
salt
½ cup olive oil
juice of 1 lemon
freshly ground black pepper
4 guinea hen breasts,
   including the drumstick
2 tbsp unsalted butter
2 large handfuls of mixed
   micro-greens
4oz (120g) Feta cheese

 ROSIN'S TIP: If you don't have leftover bread dumplings but you want a crispy coating, substitute crushed cornflakes.

CRISPY DUCK BREAST
IN A SAVORY SAUCE

Necessity really is the mother of invention. Many years ago my oven broke, and that's when I created this recipe. When you let the duck cook long enough, the meat develops a a rich flavor and the sauce produced is delicious.

> serves 4
> 1 hour + 1½ hours to cook

2 carrots
½ head of celery root
1 leek
1 orange
1 apple
2 tbsp canola oil
1 duck, about
   5lb 8oz (2.5kg),
   preferably with
   the gizzards
¼ cup tomato paste
2 sprigs of rosemary
3 bay leaves
2 cloves
10 cups red wine
6 cups vegetable or
   chicken stock
salt
sugar
3 tbsp unsalted butter, chilled
   and cut into cubes
distilled vinegar

1 Peel and dice the carrots and celery root. Dice the leek. Cut the unpeeled orange into eight pieces. Remove the seeds. Core and chop the apple.

2 Heat the oil in a Dutch oven or roasting pan. Place the gizzards, if using, the carrots, celery root, and leek in the saucepan. Brown everything over medium-high heat. Add the tomato paste and sauté for 2 minutes. Stir in the rosemary, bay leaves, cloves, and pieces of orange and apple. Add the wine and stock. Place the duck in the liquid, breast-side down, and bring to a boil. Season with salt and sugar. Simmer for 1½ hours, until cooked.

3 Remove the duck from the roasting pan, being careful not to tear the skin. Skim the fat from the cooking liquid and strain the liquid through a sieve.

Set aside half of the liquid. Place the other half in a saucepan, bring it to a boil, and reduce it to 2 cups. Beat in the chilled butter to bind the sauce. Season to taste with sugar and distilled vinegar. Keep warm.

4 Preheat the broiler. Carefully remove the breasts from the breastbone, leaving the skin intact. Carve each duck breast in half. Place the duck breasts, skin-side up, in an ovenproof frying pan. Pour enough cooking liquid into the frying pan to cover the breast meat, but leaving the skin uncovered. Place the frying pan on the middle rack of the oven. Broil the duck breasts until the skin turns golden brown. Remove the duck and divide among on plates. Serve with the sauce on the side.

ROSIN'S TIP: The Chinese have cooked duck in stock for centuries. This method has recently become popular in Germany. Leftover duck is excellent served cold. Or make rillettes—shred the meat and preserve it in the duck fat.

CHICKEN FRICASSÉE WITH SPRING VEGETABLES

Strictly speaking, this dish should be called blanquette of chicken instead of a fricassée, because the chicken is cooked in stock rather than sauce. But I'm not one to split hairs. It's a delicious dish, and the quality of the chicken makes a big difference to the overall taste.

> serves 4–6
> 1 hour + 1½ hours to cook

1 Peel and chop the celery root and 2 carrots. Slice the leek. Place the chicken in a saucepan filled with enough lightly salted water to cover the chicken by 2in (5cm). Bring to a boil and simmer over medium heat. After 30 minutes, add the celery root, carrots, leek, bay leaves, and cloves. Simmer for 40 minutes. Remove from the heat.

2 Meanwhile, prepare the vegetables. Peel and julienne the remaining carrots. Cook for 10 minutes in salted water. Remove from the water, and plunge them into ice water. Cut the asparagus into pieces. Heat the olive oil in a frying pan, add the asparagus and peas, and sauté for 5 minutes. Season to taste with salt and sugar. Set aside and keep warm.

3 To make the sauce, peel and dice the shallot. Melt 1 tablespoon of butter in a saucepan. Add the shallots and sauté until translucent. Deglaze with the white wine and 1¾ cups chicken broth. Season with salt and pepper. Bring to a boil. Reduce the liquid for 15 minutes.

4 Take the chicken out of its broth and let it cool. Remove the skin, then remove the meat from the bones. Slice the meat into bite-sized pieces. Add the remaining butter, crème fraîche, and potato starch to the sauce, then mix with a handheld blender. Season to taste with nutmeg and lemon juice. Divide the chicken among the plates. Pour the sauce over the chicken and top with the sautéed asparagus, peas, and carrots. Serve immediately.

½ celery root
5 carrots
1 leek
1 organic chicken
salt
2 bay leaves
2 cloves
1 bunch green asparagus
  spears
2 cups sugar snap peas
1 tbsp olive oil
sugar
1 shallot
7 tbsp unsalted butter
¾ cup white wine
freshly ground black pepper
¾ cup crème fraîche
¼ cup potato starch
freshly grated nutmeg
lemon juice

 ROSIN'S TIP: You can use veal instead of chicken in this recipe. Serve with either rice or mashed potatoes. Freeze unused chicken stock and use it in other dishes.

CHICKEN BREAST
WITH A CREAMY STUFFING

It's important that all the ingredients are very cold when you are making the forcemeat for the filling. Also, keep the meat and the cream in the fridge until you need them.

> serves 4
> 30 minutes + 20 minutes to cook and rest

5 skinless boneless chicken
   breasts, about 6oz (170g)
   each
⅔ cup heavy cream
salt
freshly ground black pepper
1 tbsp canola oil

1 Cut 1 chicken breast into slices ¼in (5mm) thick, cut the slices into strips and dice them. Place the cream and diced meat in the blender and purée until smooth (or cut finely as described on 115). Season liberally with salt and pepper, to taste. Using a sharp knife, cut a deep pocket into each of the remaining 4 chicken breasts. Stuff the chicken breasts with the forcemeat and firmly press the openings closed.

2 Preheat a convection oven to 325°F (160°C) or a regular oven to 350°F (175°C). Heat the oil in a ovenproof frying pan. Place the chicken breasts in the oil and fry them on each side until golden brown. Place the frying pan on the middle rack of the oven and cook for 15 minutes more. Remove the chicken breasts from the frying pan and let rest for 5 minutes. Cut them in half diagonally and serve.

ROSIN'S TIP: Poultry is lean, so the creamy stuffing keeps the chicken from drying out. If you like, add herbs, fried onions, or dried fruit to the stuffing mixture.

POACHED SALMON WITH FAVA BEAN AND RED PEPPER PURÉES

The combination of colors looks striking on the plate, and the mix of textures is also sure to please.

> **serves 4**
> **2 hours**

1 Drain the beans in a sieve. Peel and dice the onions and garlic. Heat the oil in a saucepan, add the onions and garlic, and sauté until translucent. Season to taste with salt and sugar. Deglaze with the wine. Add the beans and savory, then pour in the stock. Simmer for 10–15 minutes, until tender.

2 Strain the beans through a sieve set over a second saucepan. Reduce the liquid until it is thick. Stir in the butter. Season to taste with salt, pepper, and sugar. Add the beans to the liquid. Keep warm.

3 For the red pepper purée, quarter the peppers. Remove the seeds and pith, and chop coarsely. Peel and dice the ginger, shallot, and garlic. Heat the oil in a saucepan. Add the bell peppers, shallots, and garlic. Sauté until translucent. Add the wine, stock, ginger, and vanilla seeds and bring to a boil. Boil for 15 minutes, until the liquid has evaporated.

4 Season the liquid with salt, pepper, and sugar. Remove from the heat. Purée with a handheld blender. Push the bell pepper purée through a sieve and season to taste. Keep warm.

5 For the salmon, peel the shallots. Heat the oil in a saucepan, add the shallots, and sauté until translucent. Season to taste with salt and sugar. Add the wine, stock, bay leaf, cloves, and thyme. Simmer for 5 minutes.

6 Place the salmon in the saucepan. Remove the saucepan from the heat. Cook the salmon in the stock for 4 minutes. Turn it and cook for another 4 minutes. Keep the fish warm. Pour the poaching liquid through a sieve into a saucepan. Boil for 5 minutes. Remove the pan from the heat. Add the quark. Using a handheld blender, mix the sauce until it is thick and creamy. Divide the bell pepper purée among the plates. Place a salmon fillet on each plate. Top with the bean purée. Serve.

FAVA BEAN PURÉE
2lb 4oz (1kg) canned fava beans
2 onions
1 garlic clove
1 tbsp olive oil
salt and sugar, to taste
½ cup white wine
1 sprig of savory
4 cups chicken stock
1 tbsp chilled, unsalted butter
freshly ground black pepper

RED PEPPER PURÉE
3 red bell peppers
1in (2.5cm) fresh ginger
1 shallot
1 garlic clove
1 tbsp olive oil
½ cup white wine
2½ cups vegetable stock
seeds of 1 vanilla bean
salt, freshly ground
black pepper, and sugar, to taste

POACHED SALMON
3 shallots
1 tbsp olive oil
salt
sugar
¾ cup white wine
4 cups chicken stock
1 bay leaf
2 cloves
1 sprig of thyme
4 skinless salmon fillets, about
   7oz (200g) each
5½oz (150g) quark or sour cream

 ROSIN'S TIP: Even beginners can quickly master this salmon recipe. It works well with many kinds of fish fillet.

STEAMED MONKFISH **RAVIOLI** WITH ASIAN VEGETABLES

Ravioli doesn't always have to contain a classic spinach or meat stuffing. Filled with fish and cooked Asian-style over steam, these pasta packages are delicious little morsels.

> serves 4
> 50 minutes + 1 hour to rest + 15 minutes to steam

2 cups all-purpose flour
½ tsp salt, plus salt to taste
2 tsp olive oil
1 shallot
1 small carrot
½ zucchini
1 small red bell pepper
4 scallions
1 bunch of cilantro leaves
1 tbsp sesame oil
freshly ground black pepper
1 large egg yolk
8 pieces boneless, skinless
    monkfish, about
    2oz (60g) each
canola oil
6 tbsp brown butter
    (see page 219)

1 Place the flour in a bowl and make a well. Add ⅔ cup hot water, the salt, and olive oil. Knead to form a smooth dough. Roll the dough into a ball and wrap in plastic wrap. Refrigerate for 1 hour.

2 To make the filling, peel and dice the shallot and carrot. Dice the zucchini. Remove the seeds and pith from the bell pepper, then dice it. Chop the scallions and cilantro leaves. Heat the sesame oil in a frying pan. Add the shallots and sauté until translucent. Add the carrot, zucchini, bell pepper, and scallions. Sauté briefly, then add the cilantro (reserving some for later). Season to taste with salt and pepper.

3 Roll out the dough to the thickness of a quarter. Use a 2in (5cm) cookie cutter to cut 16 rounds. Whisk the egg yolk in a bowl. Distribute the vegetable filling among 8 pasta rounds. Place 1 piece of monkfish on each round. Brush the edges of the dough with egg yolk and put the second 8 rounds on top of the filling. Pinch the edges together.

4 Fill a saucepan one-third full of water. Bring the water to a boil. Coat a wide-mesh sieve with canola oil and add the ravioli. Place the sieve over the boiling water and cover. Steam for 15 minutes.

5 Melt the butter in a frying pan and the gently toss the ravioli in the butter. Divide the ravioli among the plates, and sprinkle them with the reserved cilantro. Serve immediately.

ROSIN'S TIP: Use salmon or roast beef in place of monkfish. Line the steamer with fresh herbs, so they transfer their flavor to the pasta dough.

123

CRISPY PAN-FRIED
WALLEYE

I fry walleye fillets with the skin on so that they turn out both crispy and juicy. The thicker the fillet, the easier it is to prepare. Plus, a piece of thick fish is visually appealing. Always take time when preparing this delicate, delicious fish.

> **serves 4**
> **15 minutes**

1 Make two or three diagonal cuts in the fish skin, without cutting into the flesh. Put a little canola oil in a frying pan. Place the fillets, skin-side down, in the pan. Fry the fillets over medium heat until golden brown. Season to taste with salt and pepper.

2 The skin protects the delicate fish from the heat of the frying pan. When just the top layer of the fish is transparent, turn the fillets over. Season the skin to taste with salt and pepper. Remove the fillets from the frying pan. Serve immediately.

4 pieces boneless walleye
    fillet, skin on, about 3½oz
    (100g) each
canola oil
salt
freshly ground black pepper

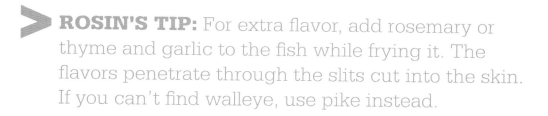

> **ROSIN'S TIP:** For extra flavor, add rosemary or thyme and garlic to the fish while frying it. The flavors penetrate through the slits cut into the skin. If you can't find walleye, use pike instead.

COD WITH BROCCOLI IN GOULASH SAUCE

This recipe is certainly unconventional, but in the best way. The flavor combination of the goulash sauce and the cod is simply unparalleled.

> serves 4
> 30 minutes

4 boneless, skinless, cod
   fillets, about 6½oz
   (180g) each
salt
freshly ground black pepper
4 tbsp clarified, unsalted
   butter (see page 219)
1 head of broccoli
1 tbsp olive oil
sugar
1 tbsp unsalted butter
1¾ cups goulash sauce
   (see page 84)

1 Preheat a convection oven to 325°F (165°C) or a regular oven to 350°F (175°C). Season the cod to taste with salt and pepper. Heat the butter in an ovenproof frying pan. Place the cod fillets in the butter and fry them on each side until golden brown. Place the frying pan on the center rack of the oven and bake for 8 minutes. Remove from the oven.

2 Separate the broccoli into florets, then cut them into thin slices. Heat the oil in a frying pan. Add the broccoli and sauté for 4 minutes. Season to taste with sugar, salt, and freshly ground pepper. Add the butter and shake the broccoli in the pan. Warm the goulash sauce. Distribute the sauce among bowls. Arrange the cod and broccoli on top. Serve immediately.

ROSIN'S TIP: Cooked fish should be always slightly translucent in the center so it retains its juiciness. For extra pep, squeeze lemon juice over the broccoli.

WHOLE **TROUT** BAKED IN FOIL

This trout dish is a winner for everyone. The play between the savory herbs and the tart lemon makes it very flavorful. For an easy, light meal, serve the fish with a green salad.

> serves 4
> 15 minutes + 30 minutes to bake

1 Cut 4 slices from the lemon and cut each in half. Chop the herbs. Peel and chop the garlic. Season the trout inside and out with salt and pepper. Place 2 tablespoons of butter, 2 half-slices of lemon, and one-quarter of the herbs and garlic in the cavity of each trout.

2 Preheat a convection oven to 350°F (175°C) or a regular oven to 375°F (190°C). Prepare four large pieces of aluminum foil and drizzle olive oil over each one. Place 1 trout in the middle of each piece of foil. Fold the foil over the fish and close tightly. Arrange the packages on a baking sheet. Place the baking sheet on the center rack of the oven and bake for 30 minutes. Remove from the oven. To serve, arrange the trout, still in the foil, on plates. Open the foil at the table.

1 organic lemon
⅓ cup mixed herbs (parsley, rosemary, cilantro, and chervil)
1 garlic clove
4 fresh, cleaned trout, about 4–6oz (120–180g) each
salt
freshly ground black pepper
3 tbsp unsalted butter
olive oil

> **ROSIN'S TIP:** Use a sharp knife to chop fresh herbs so you don't crush them, since crushing diminishes the flavor.

129

PAN-FRIED **SOLE** IN BUTTER

This is the classic way of preparing fish, one that can be used with both expensive fish like sole and with more affordable types of fish, such as trout, arctic char, and whitefish.

> **serves 4**
> **25 minutes**

⅓ cup sliced almonds
1 bunch of chervil
4 lemons
2 tbsp unsalted butter
2 tbsp sugar
⅓ cup all-purpose flour
7 tbsp clarified, unsalted
   butter (see page 219)
8 sole fillets, about 3oz
   (90g) each
salt
freshly ground black pepper
⅓ cup croutons

1 In a dry frying pan, dry-roast the almonds until golden brown. Set aside. Chop the chervil. Peel the lemons and cut them into segments. Melt the butter in a frying pan, add the sugar and lemon, and shake the pan back and forth. Remove from the heat.

2 Scatter the flour on a plate. Heat the clarified butter in a second frying pan. Season the sole with salt and pepper to taste, dredge the fillets in the flour, and shake off any excess flour. Place the fillets in the hot butter and fry them on each side for 30 seconds, until crisp. Remove from the pan, drain on paper towels, then arrange on plates.

3 Warm the lemon segments and add the chervil. Divide the lemon among the fillets. Sprinkle the almonds and croutons over the top. Serve.

> **ROSIN'S TIP:** To fillet fish, make a small cut in the skin between the tail and the end of the fillets. Hold the cut in simmering water for 3 seconds until the skin loosens. Pull the skin from the tail to the head and remove the fillets.

PICKLED HERRING SALAD WITH CARAWAY POTATOES

For a variation on this recipe, I sometimes add a second apple—the extra fruitiness blends well with the saltiness of the fish.

> serves 4
> 25 minutes + 6 hours to marinate + 25 minutes to cook

1 Place the mayonnaise in a bowl, add the cheese, and combine. Peel and dice the shallots. Peel, core, and dice the apple. Dice the pickles. Reserve the pickle liquid. Cut the pickled herring fillets into bite-sized pieces. Add the shallots, apple, pickles, and dill to the cheese mixture and stir to combine. Season to taste with salt, pepper, and a dash of pickle liquid. Fold in the herring. Cover and refrigerate for at least 6 hours.

2 Place the potatoes, water, a generous amount of salt, and the caraway seeds in a large saucepan. Bring to a boil and cook for 25 minutes, until tender. Remove the saucepan from the heat. Drain the potatoes, then let them cool slightly. Wrap the potatoes in aluminum foil. Make a cut halfway through the middle of each potato and to open it up. Place a potato on each plate. Pile the pickled herring salad in the center. Serve.

¾ cup mayonnaise (see page 218)
½ cup fresh cheese, such as quark or ricotta cheese, or sour cream
4 shallots
1 apple
1 large dill pickle
8 pickled herring fillets
1 tbsp dill, finely chopped
salt
freshly ground black pepper
4 large Russet Burbank potatoes
1 tbsp caraway seeds

 ROSIN'S TIP: Called "matjes" in German, young herring are used to make pickled herring. Immediately after they are caught, the fish are partially cleaned and placed in brine to "ripen." Fresh pickled herring is available in May, June, and July. If you can't find fresh pickled herring, use pickled herring from the jar.

SIDE DISHES

CAULIFLOWER WITH BUTTER SAUCE

With its nutty flavor, the humble cauliflower tastes like pure bliss when served in butter sauce. My Executive Chef, Harald Schroer, shared this recipe with me 30 years ago.

> **> serves 4**
> **> 25 minutes**

2 large eggs
1 small head of cauliflower
salt
14 tbsp brown butter
   (see page 219)
1½ cups Panko bread crumbs
2 tbsp finely chopped parsley
freshly ground black pepper

1 Place the eggs in boiling water and boil for 12 minutes, until hard-boiled. Separate the cauliflower into florets. Bring salted water to a boil in a saucepan. Add the cauliflower and blanch for 5 minutes. Remove the florets and plunge them into ice-cold water. Keep the cauliflower cooking water warm.

2 Heat the brown butter in a frying pan. Add the Panko bread crumbs. Peel and chop the eggs. Add the eggs to the bread crumbs. Season with parsley leaves, salt, and pepper. Heat the cauliflower in the warm cauliflower cooking water. Divide the florets among plates, spoon the sauce over the top, and serve.

CAULIFLOWER WITH BROWN BUTTER AND BACON: Blanch the cauliflower as described in Step 1. Dice 3½oz (100g) of bacon. Peel and dice 1 shallot. Finely chop ½ cup of parsley. Melt 7 tablespoons of brown butter in a frying pan. Add the bacon and shallots and sauté until the shallots are translucent and the bacon fat has melted. Add the cauliflower florets. Season to taste with salt and pepper. Mix in the parsley and serve.

ROSIN'S TIP: Watercress can be used instead of parsley. Its spicy flavor marries well with the nuttiness of the cauliflower. Both sauces taste good with Brussels sprouts and asparagus.

LAYERED
POTATO CAKE

This is the perfect potato side dish to serve when you want to impress guests. It takes a bit of work to prepare, but it's worth the effort.

> serves 4
> 1 hour + 20 minutes to cook

1 Boil the potatoes in salted water for 20 minutes, until tender. Drain, then peel them. Press the potatoes through a potato ricer into a bowl. Beat the egg whites with 1 pinch of salt until stiff and glossy. Preheat the broiler. Line a baking sheet with parchment paper.

2 Whisk the crème fraîche, butter, and egg yolks into the potato mixture. Fold in the egg whites. Season to taste with salt and nutmeg. Spread a circle of potato mixture ½in (1cm) thick and 4in (10cm) in diameter on the parchment paper. Place the baking sheet on the upper rack of the oven and broil until the potato mixture is browned on top. Prepare and broil the next potato rounds. Stack the potato layers on top of each other as you make them. Continue making potato layers until all the mixture is used up. Trim the potato layer cake so it is even all around. Cut into four pieces and serve.

1lb 2oz (500g) Russet
   Burbank potatoes
salt
7 egg whites
3 tbsp crème fraîche
1 tbsp unsalted butter
3 egg yolks
freshly grated nutmeg

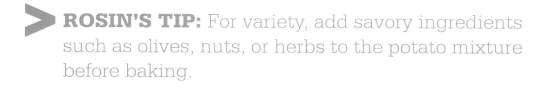

ROSIN'S TIP: For variety, add savory ingredients such as olives, nuts, or herbs to the potato mixture before baking.

FRIED
RICE BALLS

Fried rice balls might not sound like an exciting dish, but as soon as I make them, these tasty morsels are quickly devoured—which is good, because they should be eaten warm.

> **serves 4**
> **30 minutes**

5½oz (150g) Parmesan cheese
1 handful of basil leaves
3 cups cooked Basmati rice
¼ cup sweet chili sauce
2 large eggs
1½ cups Panko bread crumbs
canola oil, for frying

1 Grate the Parmesan cheese. Finely chop the basil. Combine the rice, Parmesan cheese, chili sauce, and basil. Shape 12 balls, each about 1in (2.5cm) round, from the mixture.

2 Whisk the eggs in a bowl. Scatter the bread crumbs on a plate. Heat enough oil in a deep fryer or saucepan so the rice balls float in the oil while frying. Roll the balls twice in the eggs and once in the bread crumbs. Fry in the hot oil, drain on paper towels. Serve.

> **ROSIN'S TIP:** Use up leftover meat and vegetables by adding them to the rice mixture.

STEAMED SAVOY CABBAGE ROLLS

I regularly serve these cabbage rolls as passed hors d'oevres at big events and receptions. They also make a good accompaniment to pan-fried meat or fish. They are a little complicated to make, so may require some practice.

> **serves 4**
> **1 hour**

1 Blanch the Savoy cabbage leaves in boiling salted water for 3 minutes. Remove from the water, then plunge them into ice water. Set aside.

2 Peel and dice the shallots. Melt the butter in a large frying pan. Sweat the shallots in the butter until translucent. Remove the core of the cabbage and slice it into strips. Add the cabbage to the shallots and sauté for 2 minutes. Deglaze with white wine and stir in the crème fraîche. Drain the cabbage in a sieve, reserving the liquid. Return the liquid to the frying pan. Simmer gently until the liquid is thick and creamy. Add more crème fraîche, to taste. Remove from the heat, add the cabbage to the sauce, and combine. Season to taste with salt and nutmeg.

3 Cut the leaf ribs of the cabbage leaves into V-shapes. Fold the leaves together. Place a quarter of the cabbage mixture on each leaf. Fold the leaves over the filling.

4 Place a kitchen towel on your work surface. Put a cabbage bundle in the middle. Pressing lightly, use the towel to shape the cabbage rolls into balls. Serve immediately.

4 large Savoy cabbage leaves
salt
2 shallots
4 tbsp unsalted butter
1 large head of Savoy cabbage
2 tbsp white wine
4 tbsp crème fraîche
freshly grated nutmeg

 ROSIN'S TIP: Blanched vegetables are immersed in ice water to stop the cooking process. Don't skip this step—overcooked vegetables are flavorless and dull in color.

CONFIT
POTATOES

This recipe is definitely not for anyone who's counting calories or watching their fat intake. That said, the potatoes are worth every sinful bite.

> **serves 4–6**
> **40 minutes**

4 garlic cloves
2½ cups goose fat
6 peppercorns
5 bay leaves
2 sprigs of tarragon
6 sprigs of thyme
salt
freshly ground black pepper
sugar
16 baby potatoes
sea salt

1 Peel and slice the garlic cloves. Place the goose fat, garlic, peppercorns, bay leaves, tarragon, and thyme in a saucepan. Warm the fat to 175°F (80°C). Season the goose fat mixture to taste with salt, pepper, and sugar.

2 Cut the potatoes in half lengthwise and fry them in the goose fat for 20 minutes. Remove from the fat and drain on paper towels. Season to taste with sea salt and pepper and serve.

> **ROSIN'S TIP:** Confit is derived from the French word "confire," which means to boil down or conserve. In savory cooking, the term refers to cooking meat or poultry in its fat to conserve it.

RED CABBAGE WITH GOOSE FAT

I can still picture the master chef I trained under making this recipe: He would stand over the saucepan like a conductor in front of his orchestra—a pinch of this, a bit of that, and stir—unforgettable!

> **serves 4–6**
> **50 minutes + 1½ hours to cook**

1 Cut the cabbage into quarters and remove the core. Slice or grate it into thin strips. Peel and dice the onions. Peel, quarter, and core the apples.

2 Heat the goose fat in a large saucepan. Add the onions and sauté until translucent. Add the cabbage. Stir in the apple, honey, bay leaves, and cloves. Sauté for 5 minutes. Pour in the wine and stock and cover. Simmer for 1½ hours, until tender. Stir in the cranberries. Season with salt, pepper, and sugar. Serve immediately.

2 heads of red cabbage
4 onions
2 apples
½ cup goose fat
⅓ cup honey
2 bay leaves
2 cloves
3 cups red wine
4 cups vegetable stock
½ cup dried cranberries
salt
freshly ground black pepper
sugar

> **ROSIN'S TIP:** Adding distilled vinegar to the seasonings brings out the flavors even more.

CABBAGE SALAD
WITH CARAWAY SEEDS

I love caraway seeds in cabbage salad and always mix in a few. The caraway accentuates the flavors of the cabbage and also aids in digestion.

> **serves 4**
> **40 minutes + overnight to marinate**

½ head of green cabbage
2 apples
1 onion
salt
½ cup olive oil
⅔ cup apple vinegar
½ cup vegetable stock
½ cup sugar
1–2 tsp caraway seeds
freshly ground black pepper

1 Cut the cabbage into quarters and remove the core. Slice he cabbage into thin strips. Peel, core, and grate the apples. Peel and grate the onion. Combine the ingredients in a bowl along with 2 tablespoons of salt. Knead the ingredients for 10 minutes, until the cabbage softens. Add the olive oil.

2 Place the vinegar, stock, and sugar in a saucepan and bring to a boil. Pour the cooking liquid over the cabbage. Combine the ingredients, and season with caraway and a generous amount of pepper. Refriderate overnight. Season again to taste with salt, pepper, sugar, and vinegar. Serve.

ROSIN'S TIP: An electric slicer will produce evenly cut strips of cabbage.

SWABIAN
POTATO NOODLES

The southern German version of Italian gnocchi, these extremely versatile noodles go well with savory sauces and pan-fried foods and they make a lovely dessert. In Swabia, they are called "schupfnudeln" and "bubaspitzle."

> serves 4–6
> 35 minutes + 20 minutes to cook

1 Place the potatoes in a saucepan of salted water and bring to a boil. Boil for 20 minutes, until tender. Drain and peel the potatoes. Press them through a potato ricer into a bowl while still warm. Add the egg yolk and flour and combine. Season to taste with salt and nutmeg. Knead to form a smooth dough.

2 Shape the dough into a log 2½in (6cm) thick. Cut the log into ¾in (2cm) pieces. Roll the dough between the palms of your hands to form 2½in (6cm) noodles. If the dough is too sticky, work in some flour.

3 Bring a saucepan of salted water to a boil. Add the noodles. Boil for 5 minutes, until the noodles float. Meanwhile, melt the butter in a frying pan. Remove the noodles from the water and brown in the butter. Serve.

ALMOND POTATO NOODLES:
Place 2 tablespoons of sliced almonds and 1 tablespoon of butter in a frying pan and brown. Add 1 tablespoon of sugar. Stir until caramelized. Add the noodles and shake them back and forth in the almond butter. Season to taste with cinnamon and grated orange zest.

9oz (250g) Russet Burbank potatoes
salt
1 egg yolk
½ cup all-purpose flour
freshly grated nutmeg
2 tbsp unsalted butter

SWABIAN SPÄTZLE

Spätzle are egg noodles. Quick and easy to make, they absorb the sauce from roast beef well and are part of the classic Sunday lunch menu in Germany.

> **serves 4**
> **15 minutes**

salt
2 cups all-purpose flour
2 large eggs
freshly grated nutmeg
4 tbsp unsalted butter

1 Bring a saucepan of salted water to a boil. Place the flour in a bowl and make a well in the flour. Add the eggs, 1 pinch each of salt and nutmeg, and ½ cup of water. Mix with a wooden spoon until the ingredients are combined and the dough is glossy and drops slowly from the back of the spoon.

2 Place the dough in a spätzle maker and press it into the boiling water. If you don't have a spätzle maker, see the tip. The spätzle are ready once they float to the top. Melt the butter in a frying pan, add the spätzle, and shake them back and forth in the pan and fry for a few minutes.

ROSIN'S TIP: Moisten a spätzle board or cutting board. Spread 2–4 tablespoons of dough evenly over the board. Using a spätzle cutter or a paring knife, cut thin strips of dough and put them in boiling water. It may take some practice to perfect this technique.

HOMEMADE
FETTUCCINE

It can take a while to learn how to make pasta that's the right consistency every time. Once you've have tasted the difference between homemade and store-bought pasta, however, you'll agree that the extra effort is worth it.

> serves 4
> 40 minutes + 30 minutes to rest

1 Chop the parsley leaves. In a bowl, combine the flour and semolina and form a well in the middle. Break the eggs into the well and add salt. Knead the dough well. Cover the dough with a kitchen towel and refrigerate for 30 minutes.

2 Bring a saucepan of salted water to a boil. Place the dough on a lightly floured work surface and roll it out until it's the thickness of a quarter. If using a pasta machine, feed the dough through the machine. If not, cut the dough into pieces 9in (20cm) wide.

Roll them up, then cut the pieces into thin strips. Flour your hands, loosen the fettuccine strands, and spread them out on the work surface. Cook the pasta in the boiling salted for 3–5 minutes. Drain in a sieve.

3 Melt the butter in a frying pan. Add the cooked fettuccine. Season with salt, pepper, nutmeg, and parsley, and toss. Serve immediately.

1 handful of parsley leaves
3 cups all-purpose flour
1 cup semolina
4 eggs
salt
7 tbsp unsalted butter
freshly ground black pepper
freshly grated nutmeg

ORANGE
SAUERKRAUT

Sauerkraut has always been a popular winter vegetable in Germay. This is my favorite way to prepare it, and this dish tastes good warm or cold.

> serves 4
> 30 minutes

1 shallot
3 tbsp unsalted butter
14oz (400g) sauerkraut
2 bay leaves
1 clove
1¾ cups freshly squeezed
    orange juice
1 tbsp sugar
zest of 1 organic orange
salt
freshly ground black pepper

1 Peel and dice the shallot. Melt 1 tablespoon of butter in a frying pan, add the shallot, and sauté until translucent. Add the sauerkraut, bay leaves, and clove and sauté. Add 1¼ cups of orange juice and bring to a boil.

2 Boil until the orange juice has evaporated. Add the remaining butter and the sugar. Cook the sauerkraut until it is golden, adding the remaining juice a little at a time. Season the with orange zest, salt, and pepper. Serve.

ROSIN'S TIP: I suggest making this dish a day in advance because it tastes even better when it's reheated. It goes well with pan-fried fish, such as the walleye on page 125.

MASHED POTATOES
WITH OLIVE OIL

At some point I became bored with plain mashed potatoes. Then, when visiting the island of Majorca, I was served potatoes with garlic and onions, and this dish was born.

> serves 4–6
> 25 minutes + 20 minutes to cook

1 Place the potatoes and caraway seeds in a saucepan of salted water. Bring to a boil. Cook for 20 minutes, until tender.

2 Meanwhile, peel and slice the shallots. Heat 1 tablespoon of olive oil in a frying pan. Add the shallots and sauté until translucent. As soon as they begin to brown, add the sugar and stir well. Sauté until the shallots are golden brown. Deglaze with the stock.

3 Drain and peel the potatoes. Place them in a bowl and mash with a potato masher. Add the shallots and remaining olive oil and mix. Season to taste with salt and lemon juice. Serve immediately.

14oz (400g) Russet Burbank
    potatoes
1 tsp caraway seeds
salt
8 shallots
½ cup olive oil
2 tbsp sugar
¼ cup vegetable stock
sea salt
lemon juice

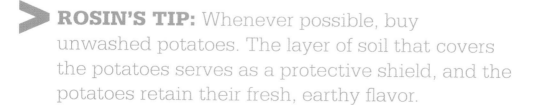

> **ROSIN'S TIP:** Whenever possible, buy unwashed potatoes. The layer of soil that covers the potatoes serves as a protective shield, and the potatoes retain their fresh, earthy flavor.

PEA AND MINT PURÉE WITH BROWN BUTTER

This recipe calls for a bit of experience on the part of the cook, so don't get discouraged if it takes you a few tries to get the hang of it.

> **serves 4**
> **40 minutes**

2 shallots
7 tablespoons of brown butter
   (see page 219)
4½ cups peas (fresh or frozen)
3¼ cups vegetable stock
3½oz (100g) mint leaves
lemon juice
sugar
salt

1 Peel and dice the shallots. Heat 1 tablespoon of brown butter in a frying pan. Add the shallots and sauté until translucent. Add the peas. Pour in the stock and bring to a boil. Simmer until the liquid is reduced by half and the peas are tender. Strain through a sieve. Reserve the liquid.

2 Using a handheld blender, purée the peas, adding the cooking liquid a little at a time until the purée is creamy. Rub the purée through a sieve to remove any pea hulls.

3 If the purée is too runny, return it to the frying pan continue to cook. Chop the mint. Stir the remaining brown butter and mint into the purée. Season the purée to taste with lemon juice, sugar, and salt. Serve immediately.

ROSIN'S TIP: Prepare the pea and mint purée last and serve it right away so its aroma doesn't dissipate. Fried scallops with pea and mint purée is a perfect appetizer for an elegant dinner.

CRISPY
POTATO PANCAKES

Potato pancakes are one of my favorite side dishes. For full flavor, they should be fried until they are as crisp as potato chips. This mixture can also serve as the basis for rösti.

> serves 4
> 45 minutes

1 Peel and grate the potatoes and shallots. Combine in a bowl. Season to taste with salt and pepper. Let stand for 5 minutes. Use a kitchen towel to squeeze the liquid from the grated potatoes. Work in the egg and flour.

2 Heat the oil in a frying pan. Using a tablespoon, cut small portions from the potato mixture. Place them in the frying pan and press flat. Fry on each side until crispy. Remove the potato pancakes from the frying pan and drain them on paper towels. Repeat until the potato mixture is used up. Stack them in little towers and serve.

14oz (400g) Russet Burbank
   potatoes
2 shallots
salt
freshly ground black pepper
1 egg
3 tbsp all-purpose flour
3 tbsp canola oil

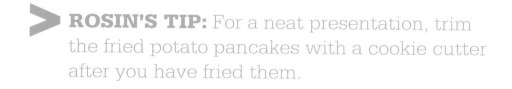

ROSIN'S TIP: For a neat presentation, trim the fried potato pancakes with a cookie cutter after you have fried them.

CLASSIC **NAPKIN DUMPLINGS**

Traditionally, dumplings were wrapped in napkins or linen cloths before cooking—hence the name. This method for making dumplings originated in Upper Franconia and came via Austria. The dumplings can be made ahead of time, plus leftovers can be sliced and pan-fried.

> serves 4
> 35 minutes + 15 minutes to rest + 1 hour to cook

1 bunch of parsley
1 onion
4 tbsp unsalted butter
6 day-old bread rolls
1¼ cups milk
2 egg yolks
1 egg
¾ cup all-purpose flour
freshly grated nutmeg
salt
freshly ground pepper

1 Chop the parsley. Peel and dice the onion. Melt the butter in a frying pan, add the onion and sauté until translucent. Cut up the rolls, place them in a bowl and add the butter-and-onion mixture. Add the milk, egg yolks, egg, flour, and parsley. Combine well. Season, then let rest for 15 minutes.

2 In a saucepan, bring water to a boil. Place the dumpling mixture on a sheet of heat-resistant plastic wrap and roll it into a firm log. Place the log in the boiling water. Poach the dumpling in barely simmering water for 1 hour. Remove from the water, unwrap, and cut into slices to serve.

BREAD DUMPLINGS

For me, a meal made from leftover bread dumplings is a feast. To make this dish, cut the dumplings into cubes and fry them. Break an egg over the top, serve with dill pickles on the side, and that's it... you have a lovely meal.

> serves 4
> 30 minutes + 20 minutes to rest + 20 minutes to cook

1 shallot
2 slices uncooked ham
2 tbsp unsalted butter
6 day-old bread rolls
½ cup milk
salt
1 bunch of flat-leaf parsley
3 eggs
freshly grated nutmeg

1 Peel and dice the shallot. Dice the ham. Melt 1 tablespoon of the butter in a frying pan. Add the ham and shallot and sauté until the shallot is translucent. Cut the rolls into cubes. Warm the milk and remaining butter in a saucepan and pour it over the bread. Add the ham and shallots and combine. Rest for 10 minutes.

2 Bring a saucepan of salted water to a boil. Chop the parsley leaves. Work the eggs and parsley into the bread mixture. Season to taste with salt and nutmeg and rest for 10 minutes. Moisten your hands, then shape 8 dumplings from the mixture. Place the dumplings in the water and poach for 20 minutes.

SQUASH PURÉE
WITH PICKLED GINGER

Although pickled ginger is milder than fresh ginger, it's still zingy enough to give this squash purée a nice pep.

> serves 4–6
> 1 hour

1 Slice the top and bottom from the squash. Cut it in half, remove the seeds, and cut into cubes. Peel and chop the onion. Place the butter in a large saucepan and melt it over medium heat. Add the onion and sauté until translucent. Add the squash to the saucepan. Combine will and simmer.

2 Once the liquid has evaporated, add 2 tablespoons of sugar and the stock. Bring to a boil. Stirring regularly, reduce the heat and simmer over low heat for 25 minutes. When the liquid has evaporated, remove the pan from the heat. Purée the squash with a handheld blender. Season to taste with salt, pepper, sugar, and chopped pickled ginger. Serve.

1 Hokkaido squash, about 4lb 8oz (2kg)
1 onion
9 tbsp unsalted butter
sugar
4 cups vegetable stock
salt
freshly ground black pepper
2 tbsp pickled ginger

 ROSIN'S TIP: If you don't find Hokkaido squash, use butternut squash instead. Butternut squash needs to be peeled.

PEARL BARLEY RISOTTO
WITH PECORINO CHEESE

Pearl barley has been used in cooking for centuries, especially in soups and stews. This dish is wonderfully creamy and has a very tender bite. And it's a great alternative to rice.

> serves 4
> 20 minutes + 40 minutes to cook

1 shallot
1 tbsp unsalted butter
1 cup pearl barley
1 bay leaf
1 clove
1 cup white wine
1 cup vegetable stock
2oz (60g) Pecorino
    Romano cheese

1 Peel and dice the shallot. Melt the butter in a saucepan. Add the shallots, and sauté until translucent. Add the barley and sauté briefly. Add the bay leaf and clove. Deglaze with the white wine and pour in the vegetable stock. Simmer for 10 minutes.

2 Remove the barley from the heat and let it swell for 30 minutes. Grate the Pecorino Romano. Remove the bay leaf and clove from the barley, stir in the Pecorino cheese, and serve.

ROSIN'S TIP: Pearl barley risotto is easier to cook than rice risotto because it doesn't need to be stirred constantly. Parmesan cheese can be substituted for Pecorino Romano. This dish pairs brilliantly with fried mushrooms.

BOSTON LETTUCE
WITH CREAMY DRESSING

This side salad is a classic. It tastes delicious, whether it's served with fish, pan-fried meat, or even simple boiled potatoes.

> **serves 4**
> **15 minutes**

1 Cut the lettuce hearts into quarters and remove the cores. Peel and dice the shallots and garlic. Heat the olive oil in a frying pan, add the shallots and garlic and sauté until translucent.

2 Remove the pan from the heat and add the cream. Season to taste with salt, sugar, and lemon juice. Pour the mixture into a tall container and blend with a handheld blender until foamy. Arrange the lettuce hearts on plates and top with the dressing. Serve.

2 Boston lettuce hearts
2 shallots
½ garlic clove
1 tbsp olive oil
2 cups heavy cream
salt
sugar
juice of 1 lemon

ROSIN'S TIP: Don't be put off by the notion of a "sweet" salad. The shallots and garlic provide a savory counterbalance to the sweetness of the sugar. The creamy dressing is also delicious with romaine lettuce.

DESSERTS

CARAMELIZED
LIME SQUARES

The recipe for these squares actually originated in England, but I have the recipe from my aunt. The squares taste best fresh out of the oven—pure lime flavor with a buttery echo.

> **makes 16 bars**
> **45 minutes + 1 hour to cool + 2 hours to bake**

2 cups all-purpose flour
9 tbsp unsalted butter, chilled,
    and cut into cubes
7 eggs
1 pinch of salt
⅔ cup heavy cream
⅔ cup sugar
juice of 8 limes
zest of 3 organic limes
confectioners' sugar, for
    dusting

1 Combine the flour, butter, 1 egg, and the salt and knead into a smooth dough. Roll the dough into a ball, wrap it in plastic wrap, and refrigerate for at least 1 hour.

2 Preheat a convection oven to 350°F (170°C) or a conventional oven to 375°F (185°C). Roll out the dough. Line an 8in (20cm) square cake pan with the dough. Form an edge with the dough, making sure the sides of the pan are covered so that filling doesn't leak during baking. Place the pan on the center rack of the oven and blind bake for 15 minutes (see page 16). Remove the pan and the dried beans. Reduce the convection oven temperature to 225°F (110°C) or the conventional oven to 250°F (120°C).

3 Meanwhile, to make the filling, beat the cream until stiff. Beat the remaining 6 eggs and the sugar for 6 minutes, until foamy. Add the lime juice and zest. Fold in the whipped cream. Spread the filling over the still-hot crust. Place the cake pan on the center rack of the oven and bake for 2 hours. Remove from the oven, let cool, and remove from the pan.

4 Before serving, slice the cake into squares and dust with confectioners' sugar. Caramelize the sugar with a kitchen torch. Serve immediately.

ROSIN'S TIP: The slightly bitter caramel layer provides a lovely contrast to the soft sweet filling. The squares taste wonderful served with Maracuja fruit or passion fruit.

WARM PEACHES
IN PARCHMENT PAPER

We serve this warm fruit dessert at the restaurant with raw milk cheese. When you open the parchment paper and the peach aroma wafts up your nose, it is a revelation.

> serves 4
> 40 minutes

1 Preheat a convection oven to 350°F (180°C) or a conventional oven to 375°F (190°C). Slice the lemongrass into small pieces. Cut the peaches in half lengthwise and remove the pits. Make four cuts into each peach so they better absorb the flavors of the spices. Arrange 4 sheets of parchment paper—each 8 x 10in (20 × 25cm)—on a baking sheet.

2 Distribute the cloves, star anise, and Kaffir lime leaves evenly over the parchment paper. Place the peach halves, cut-side down, on top of the spices. Brush the peaches with the honey. Place 1 sheet of parchment paper over each of the peach halves. Fold the paper in at the edges. Bake the peaches on the center rack of the oven for 12–15 minutes. Remove from the oven. Serve them in the paper and open the bundles at the table.

2 stalks of lemongrass
2 peaches
8 cloves
8 star anise
10 Kaffir lime leaves
4 tsp honey

> **ROSIN'S TIP:** Baking in parchment paper ensures that the flavors penetrate into the peaches and the fruit stays moist. Use ripe peaches for this recipe. If you like, add a sprig of rosemary to the spices.

SALTED
VANILLA ICE CREAM
WITH STRAWBERRIES

Our grandmothers knew that cake batter tastes better when it includes a pinch of salt. I used to get annoyed when the vanilla flavor of creams and ice creams would be too weak—then I remembered my grandmother's tip of adding salt.

> **> serves 6**
> **> 35 minutes + cooling time**

VANILLA ICE CREAM
½ cup milk
1 cup heavy cream
seeds of 1 vanilla bean
4 egg yolks
½ cup sugar
1 pinch of sea salt
½ cup whiskey

STRAWBERRIES
7oz (200g) strawberries
2 tbsp confectioners' sugar
lemon juice
4 mint leaves

1 Place the milk, cream, and vanilla seeds in a saucepan and bring to a boil. Beat the egg yolks and sugar in a metal bowl. Stirring constantly, add the milk and cream mixture to the egg mixture.

2 Set the bowl over a saucepan of simmering water. Add the sea salt and whiskey. Whisk until the cream passes the "rose test" (see below). Strain everything through a sieve and let cool. Place the mixture into an ice cream maker. Following the manufacturer's instructions, churn the cream until it turns into creamy ice cream. Place the ice cream in the freezer. Remove from the freezer 5 minutes before serving.

3 Hull and quarter the strawberries. Caramelize the confectioners' sugar in a frying pan, add the strawberries, and shake them back and forth briefly in the caramel. Remove the pan from the heat and drizzle lemon juice over the strawberries. Scoop small portions of the ice cream and serve with the strawberries. Garnish with mint leaves. Serve immediately.

ROSIN'S TIP: Use the "rose test" when cooking creams over simmering water. Whisk cream vigorously over simmering water until it is thick and creamy. Dip a wooden spoon in the cream and blow on the back of the spoon. Once the cream forms rose-shaped "petals" it is ready.

CHERRY PARFAIT
WITH LEMONGRASS

This is a delicious ice-cream dessert, and one that you don't need an ice-cream maker to create. The lemongrass, clove, and cherry flavors unite to form a perfect trio.

> **serves 6**
> **1 hour + 1 day to cool**

1 Finely slice the lemongrass. Place the cherry juice, cloves, and lemongrass in a saucepan and bring to a boil. Simmer and reduce the liquid to 2 cups. Remove from the heat. Sprinkle gelatin over the top, then whisk until dissolved.

2 Place the egg yolks and sugar in a metal bowl. Set the bowl over a saucepan of simmering water. Whisk for 5 minutes. Add the cherry juice and cherry syrup and whisk for 5 minutes more to form a smooth cream. Remove the bowl from the saucepan and strain through a sieve into a bowl.

3 Place the cream mixture in the refrigerator. In separate bowls, beat the cream and crème fraîche until stiff. When the cherry mixture starts to set, fold the cherry cream and crème fraîche together. Line a loaf pan with plastic wrap and pour the mixture into the pan. Freeze for at least 1 day.

4 Before serving, remove the parfait from the freezer and place it in the fridge for 5 minutes to temper it. Turn out the parfait onto a platter and remove the wrap. Cut the cherry parfait into thick slices. Serve on chilled plates.

3½oz (100g) lemongrass
4 cups cherry juice
5 cloves
2 tbsp unflavored gelatin
6 egg yolks
½ cup sugar
½ cup cherry syrup
1¼ cups heavy cream
1¼ cups crème fraîche

LEMON CREAM
JELLY ROLL

Serving cake for dessert is a tradition that comes from France and Italy. This creamy lemon jelly roll is also perfect with afternoon coffee.

> serves 6
> 1½ hours + 4 hours to refrigerate

FOR THE SPONGE CAKE
½ cup sugar
3 eggs
3 egg yolks
1 tsp pure vanilla extract
½ tsp baking powder
½ cup all-purpose flour

FOR THE LEMON CREAM
2 organic lemons
3 eggs
⅓ cup sugar
1½ tbsp unflavored
    powdered gelatin
½ cup heavy cream
salt

FOR SERVING
2¼ cups almonds
confectioners' sugar, for
    dusting

1 To make the cake, preheat the oven to 325°F (160°C). Line a rimmed 16 × 12in (40 ×30cm) baking sheet with parchment paper. Sprinkle 3 tbsp of sugar over a second identical baking sheet. Beat the eggs, egg yolks, and remaining sugar for 5 minutes, until foamy. Add the vanilla extract and beat for 3 minutes. Sift the flour and baking powder together and fold into the egg mixture. Spread the mixture evenly over the parchment paper. Place the baking sheet on the center rack of the oven and bake for 8 minutes. Remove the cake from the baking sheet immediately after taking it out of the oven. Invert it onto the baking sheet covered with sugar. Peel off the parchment paper. Let cool.

2 To make the lemon cream, juice and zest the lemons. Separate the eggs. Beat the egg yolks with 5 tablespoons of hot water until foamy. Sprinkle in the sugar a little at a time. Continue until the mixture is creamy, then stir in the lemon juice and zest. Mix in the gelatin. Let cool.

3 Chop and dry-roast the almonds in a frying pan until golden brown. Set aside. Beat the egg whites with 1 pinch of salt until stiff. Whip the cream until stiff. When the lemon mixture begins to set, fold in the egg whites and whipped cream. Spread the lemon cream over the cake. Roll up the cake from its longest side. Refrigerate for 4 hours. Roll the jelly roll in the almonds, dust with confectioners' sugar, and slice. Arrange the slices on plates. Serve.

> **ROSIN'S TIP:** Cut the jelly roll with a moistened knife so the cake doesn't stick to the knife and the slices are neat.

BRAISED
FIGS IN CASSIS

These figs in Cassis are a perfect accompaniment to the mousse on page 181.
At the restaurant, we often serve them with raw milk cheese as well.

> **serves 4**
> **20 minutes + 40 minutes to cook**

1 Preheat a convection oven to 325°F (160°C) or a conventional oven to 350°F (175°C). Place the sugar in a saucepan and caramelize over medium heat. Make a shallow cut in each fig. Place the figs, cut-side down, into the caramel. Deglaze with the Cassis. Add the cinnamon and clove. Place the saucepan on the center rack of the oven. Braise for 30 minutes.

2 Remove the saucepan from the oven. Take the figs out of the liquid. Discard the cinnamon and clove. Place the liquid in a saucepan and boil for 10 minutes, until the liquid is thick and syrupy. Divide the figs among the plates, drizzle with syrup, and serve.

½ cup sugar
12 figs
1¼ cups Cassis
1 cinnamon stick
1 clove

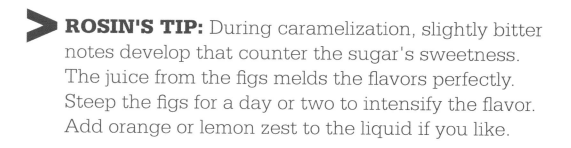

> **ROSIN'S TIP:** During caramelization, slightly bitter notes develop that counter the sugar's sweetness. The juice from the figs melds the flavors perfectly. Steep the figs for a day or two to intensify the flavor. Add orange or lemon zest to the liquid if you like.

CLASSIC
HERRENCREME

In the eighties, herrencreme was regularly served in German homes as dessert for Sunday lunch. Its popularity has declined, which is a pity. I'd love to see this custom revived.

> **> serves 4–6**
> **> 40 minutes + 1 hour to refrigerate**

4 cups milk
5 tbsp sugar
seeds of 1 vanilla bean
½ cup cornstarch
4 eggs
3½oz (100g) dark chocolate
½ cup heavy cream
½ cup rum

1 Place the milk, 4 tablespoons of sugar, the vanilla seeds, and cornstarch in a saucepan and bring to a boil. Remove from the heat and let cool. Separate the eggs. Place the egg yolks and remaining sugar in a bowl and beat for 5 minutes. Gradually mix the egg mixture into the milk mixture. Cover and refrigerate for at least 1 hour.

2 Grate the chocolate. Place the cream and egg whites in separate bowls and beat each until stiff. Remove the pudding mixture from the refrigerator. Whisk until the pudding is smooth. Mix in the rum and chocolate. Fold in the cream, then the egg whites. Divide the pudding among dessert bowls. Serve immediately.

ROSIN'S TIP: Vary this recipe by replacing the dark chocolate with coated candies, chocolate-covered coffee beans, or candied fruit.

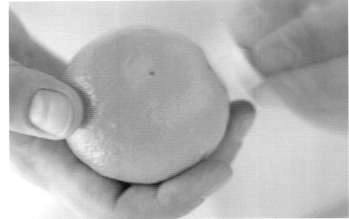

VANILLA
MANDARIN MOUSSE

The taste of this dessert is subtle, yet fantastic. Using sugar cubes to rub the zest off the mardarins requires patience, but the full flavor this delivers is worth the effort.

> **easy**
> **45 minutes + 3 hours to refrigerate**

1 Using the sugar cubes, gently rub the peel off the mandarins. Juice the 9 organic mandarins. Place a quarter of the juice, the sugar cubes, and the vanilla seeds in a saucepan and heat. Sprinkle the gelatin over the juice mixture. Add the remaining mandarin juice, lemon juice, and sour cream. Stir to combine. Divide among four glass jars. Refrigerate for 3 hours.

2 Peel 4 mandarins, pull apart the segments, and place them on top of the now firm mandarin mousse. Juice the remaining 2 mandarins. Stir the mandarin juice with honey, to taste, and drizzle it over the top of each dessert. Serve immediately.

1¼ cups sugar cubes
15 mandarins, 9 of them
    organic
seeds of 1 vanilla bean
1½ tbsp unflavored gelatin
    powder
juice of 2 lemons
1¼ cups sour cream
honey

> **ROSIN'S TIP:** The cream should be eaten immediately, before it loses its flavor and aroma.

SWEET RAVIOLI WITH MARZIPAN FILLING AND YOGURT SAUCE

Pasta isn't just a savory dish; it can be sweet as well. Our grandmothers knew this, and they cooked pasta in milk, sprinkled it with cinnamon sugar, and served it with compote. Here is an elegant variation on this theme.

> serves 4–6
> 1 hour + 30 minutes to cool

FOR THE RAVIOLI

11 tbsp unsalted butter, at room temperature
3 cups all-purpose flour
5 eggs
2 pinches of salt
1 pinch of confectioners' sugar
seeds of 1 vanilla bean
1 cup sliced almonds
5½oz (150g) marzipan
¾ cup chocolate-hazelnut spread
1 egg yolk
1 tsp granulated sugar

FOR THE YOGURT SAUCE

1 organic lemon
3¼ cups plain yogurt
seeds of 1 vanilla bean
⅔ cup confectioners' sugar

1 To make the ravioli dough, place the butter, flour, eggs, salt, confectioners' sugar, and the seeds of 1 vanilla bean in a bowl and combine. Knead to form a smooth dough. Roll the dough into a ball, wrap it in plastic wrap, and refrigerate for 30 minutes.

2 To make the filling, dry-roast the almonds in a frying pan. Remove from the heat and let cool. Knead the almonds, marzipan, and chocolate-hazelnut spread until well combined. Set aside.

3 To make the yogurt sauce, juice and zest the lemon. Combine the yogurt, lemon juice, zest, and vanilla seeds. Sift the confectioners' sugar over the mixture and whisk it in.

4 Roll out the dough to ⅛in (3mm) thickness. Cut 24 rounds using a 2in (5cm) cookie cutter. Distribute the filling among 12 rounds of dough. Brush the egg yolk over the edges of the dough. Cover each dough round with another round. Squeeze the edges firmly to seal.

5 Place the granulated sugar in a saucepan of water and bring to a simmer. Slide the ravioli into the water and cook for 5 minutes. Remove from the water and pat dry with paper towels. Divide the yogurt sauce among plates and top with the ravioli. Serve immediately.

ROSIN'S TIP: Either use a pasta machine to roll out the dough or roll it between layers of plastic wrap. Serve the ravioli immediately after cooking so it is firm to the bite.

SEMOLINA PUDDING
WITH MARINATED PLUMS

Combining sweet, rich flavors, this dish is a classic German dessert.
If you want to serve it to children, simply omit the alcohol.

> **serves 4–6**
> **1½ hours + 4 hours to marinate**

1 To make the marinated plums, remove the pits and quarter the plums. Slice the lemongrass. Place the sugar in a saucepan and stir over medium heat until it caramelizes. Add the lemongrass, cloves, and vanilla seeds, and stir. Deglaze with the plum juice and reduce the liquid to ¾ cup. Strain the liquid through a sieve and add the plum brandy. Add the plums and marinate for 4 hours.

2 To make the pudding, place the milk (reserving 3 tablespoons), sugar, vanilla bean, and salt into a saucepan. Bring to a boil. Remove the vanilla bean. Stir in

the semolina and cook over low heat for 10 minutes. Juice and zest the lemon. Separate the eggs. Beat the egg whites until stiff. Whisk the egg yolks and remaining milk until smooth. Remove the semolina from the heat. Stir in the egg and milk mixture. Fold in the egg whites, lemon juice, and zest.

3 Drain the plums through a sieve set over a saucepan. Place the saucepan on the stove. Boil the marinade until it has thickened. Add the plums and warm them briefly in the liquid. Divide the pudding among bowls, then add the warm plums. Serve immediately.

PLUMS
12 plums
2 stalks of lemongrass
¼ cup sugar
5 cloves
seeds of 2 vanilla beans
3¼ cups plum juice
2 tsp plum brandy

SEMOLINA PUDDING
4 cups milk
½ cup sugar
1 vanilla bean
1 pinch of salt
1 cup semolina
½ organic lemon
2 eggs

 ROSIN'S TIP: The beaten egg whites are what make the semolina mixture light and fluffy. Gently folding in the egg whites ensures that the beaten-in air is retained.

PANCAKES
WITH CARAMELIZED ORANGES

Orange is a wonderful flavor transporter. The combination of saffron, cloves, and vanilla teases a fabulous spectrum of flavor from the orange.

> **serves 4**
> **50 minutes**

PANCAKES

1 egg white
1 egg
1 pinch of salt
¾ cup all-purpose flour
2 tbsp sugar
½ tsp pure vanilla extract
½ cup milk
¼ cup carbonated
   mineral water
zest of 1 organic lemon
canola oil
confectioners' sugar, for
   dusting

ORANGES

3 organic oranges
2 tbsp sugar
3 cloves
1½ tsp saffron threads
seeds of ½ vanilla bean
2 tsp Grand Marnier

1 To make the pancake batter, beat the egg white until stiff. Place the egg, salt, flour, sugar, vanilla extract, milk, mineral water, and lemon peel in a bowl. Stir together to make a thick batter. Fold in the egg white. Let rest for 10 minutes.

2 Meanwhile, to make the caramelized oranges, zest the oranges, cut out the segments, and catch the juice in a bowl. Caramelize the sugar in a saucepan. Add the cloves and saffron and deglaze with the orange juice. Add the orange zest and vanilla seeds. Reduce the liquid until it is thick and syrupy. Toss the orange segments in the Grand Marnier. Strain the syrup into the bowl containing the orange segments.

3 Heat a nonstick frying pan and oil it lightly. Add the batter to the pan and fry 4 large, or 8 small, pancakes over low heat. The pancakes should not become brown, but remain as lightly colored as possible. Arrange the pancakes on plates. Top with the orange segments and syrup. Dust with confectioners' sugar and serve.

ROSIN'S TIP: The bubbles in the mineral water bring air into the batter, making the pancakes fluffy. Serve with the vanilla ice cream on page 178.

ROSIN'S TIP:
This recipe calls for a lot of batter because the apple rings have to be submerged in it so they are thoroughly coated. Freeze leftover batter and defrost it in the fridge before reusing.

FRIED APPLE RINGS
IN THREE KINDS OF BATTER

When I prepare this dessert, childhood memories of batter-eating binges in the kitchen come to mind. Today, just like then, I love the combination of the tartness of the apples and the warm roasted smell of the fried batter.

> serves 6
> 1 hour

1 To make the cornflake and almond batter, dry-roast the almonds in a frying pan until golden brown. Add the cornflakes and combine. Remove from the heat and let cool. Coarsely chop the mixture. Place the eggs, egg yolks, and sugar in a bowl and beat for 5 minutes, until foamy. Sift the flour and fold it in a little at a time. Fold in the cornflake and almond mixture. Set aside.

2 To make the cake batter, place the eggs, egg yolks, and sugar in a bowl. Beat for 5 minutes, until foamy. Sift the flour and cornstarch together. Fold them into the egg mixture. Set aside.

3 To make the beer batter, separate the eggs. Beat the egg whites until stiff. Place the flour, beer, and salt in a bowl and mix until smooth. Stir in the egg yolks. Fold in the egg whites. Set aside.

4 Heat the canola oil in a deep fryer to 340°F (170°C). Peel and core the apples. Cut the apples into ½in (1cm) slices. Divide the apple rings into three groups. Coat each group in one batter and fry until crisp. Repeat with the remaining apple rings. Drain on paper towels. Divide the apple rings among plates, dust with confectioners' sugar, and serve warm.

CORNFLAKE AND ALMOND BATTER
½ cup sliced almonds
¾ cup cornflakes
4 eggs
2 egg yolks
⅓ cup sugar
½ cup all-purpose flour

CAKE BATTER
8 eggs
3 egg yolks
⅔ cup sugar
1 cup all-purpose flour
3 tbsp cornstarch

BEER BATTER
8 eggs
4 cups all-purpose flour
4 cups lager beer
1 pinch of salt

APPLE RINGS
canola oil
4 apples
confectioners' sugar, for dusting

FRENCH TOAST
WITH YOGURT FOAM

A dessert that uses up leftovers is something I really treasure. You can also make the French toast with brioche, braided bread loaf, or white bread.

> **serves 4**
> **25 minutes**

1 egg
¾ cup milk
4 slices raisin bread
4 tbsp unsalted butter
⅓ cup cinnamon sugar
1 organic lemon
¾ cup Ayran
1 tbsp honey

1 Whisk the egg and milk together. Soak the bread in the egg mixture. Melt the butter in a frying pan. Add the bread and fry until golden brown. Remove the bread and drain on paper towels. Arrange the French toast on plates. Sprinkle with cinnamon sugar.

2 Zest and juice the lemon. Using a handheld blender, beat the Ayran, lemon juice, lemon zest, and honey until foamy. Serve the yogurt foam with the French toast.

ROSIN'S TIP: The Turkish yogurt drink Ayran gives this French toast a fresh touch. To make it yourself, place 2¼ cups of chilled yogurt (at least 3.5 percent fat) in a bowl. Add 1 pinch of salt and a few squeezes of lemon juice. Beat until foamy, gradually adding 2 cups of water.

ROSIN'S TIP: Kombucha is made with the kombucha tea fungus from sweetened black or green tea. The sugar kickstarts the fermentation process. Depending on the ambient temperature, it takes 1–2 weeks of fermentation before the sparkling drink is ready. You can buy ready-made kombucha or substitute cherry juice.

ORANGE WAFFLES
WITH KOMBUCHA CHERRIES

Nothing beats the aroma of freshly made waffles. A cherry pitter like the one shown comes in handy when pitting the cherries. The compote served on the side can be flavored with rum, brandy, or whiskey.

> serves 4
> 1½ hours + 2 hours to marinate + 30 minutes to rest

1 To make kombucha cherries, pit the cherries and place them in a bowl. Caramelize the sugar in a saucepan. Add the vanilla seeds, cloves, and Kaffir lime leaves. Deglaze with the kombucha and reduce the liquid to 2 cups. In a small bowl, mix the cornstarch with a bit of kombucha. Stir into the saucepan. Boil the liquid until the sauce has thickened. Strain through a sieve onto the cherries. Let the cherries marinate for about 2 hours. Warm them before serving.

2 To make the orange waffles, zest and juice the oranges. Place the butter and sugar in a bowl. Beat for 8 minutes, until creamy. Add the eggs and continue. Sift the flour, cornstarch, and baking powder over the egg mixture and beat it in. Add the mineral water, orange zest, and orange juice, and stir. Let the batter rest for 30 minutes. Cook the waffles according to the instructions given with your waffle iron. Divide the waffles among plates and dust with confectioners' sugar. Serve with the warm kombucha cherries.

KOMBUCHA CHERRIES

4 cups cherries
¾ cup sugar
seeds of 1 vanilla bean
5 cloves
20 Kaffir lime leaves
4 cups kombucha
2 tbsp cornstarch

ORANGE WAFFLES

2 organic oranges
11 tbsp unsalted butter
¾ cup sugar
4 eggs
1 cup all-purpose flour
1 cup cornstarch
1 tsp baking powder
½ cup mineral water
confectioners' sugar, for
   dusting

SAFFRON PEARS
WITH RICE PUDDING

Pears Belle Helene, a standard dessert of the postwar period, is newly interpreted here. Instead of serving the pears with vanilla ice cream and chocolate sauce, I've paired them with saffron, spices, and rice pudding, revealing a new dimension to the flavor of pears.

> serves 4
> 1 hour + 1 hour to cook + 8 hours to marinate

SAFFRON PEARS
4 stalks of lemongrass
1 cup sugar
seeds of 4 vanilla beans
10 Kaffir lime leaves
6 star anise
10 cloves
2 tsp saffron threads
8½ cups white wine
4 pears
½ organic lemon
¼ cup crème fraîche

RICE PUDDING
3 cups milk
1 cup long grain rice
5 tsp sugar
seeds of 1 vanilla bean
1 pinch of salt
1 cinnamon stick

1 To make the saffron pears, slice the lemongrass finely. Place the sugar in a saucepan and caramelize it. Add the vanilla seeds, lemongrass, Kaffir lime leaves, star anise, cloves, and saffron. Pour in the white wine and bring to a boil. Reduce the liquid to 4 cups.

2 Peel the pears and place them in a saucepan. Place a sieve over the saucepan and strain the liquid over the fruit. Place the saucepan over the heat. Simmer for 5 minutes. Remove the pears and reduce the liquid to 2 cups. Remove from the heat. Return the pears to the liquid and marinate overnight (or for at least 8 hours), turning occasionally.

3 To make the rice pudding, place the milk, rice, sugar, vanilla seeds, salt, and cinnamon stick in a saucepan and bring to a boil. Cook the rice over very low heat for 20 minutes, stirring, until it has absorbed the milk and is creamy. Remove from the heat.

4 Place ¾ cup of the poaching liquid in a saucepan. Return it to the boil and boil until syrupy. Zest and juice the lemon. Combine the liquid, zest, and lemon juice with the crème fraîche. Fold into the rice pudding. Remove the pears from the liquid. Slice off the bottom of each pear and remove the cores. Fill the pears with warm rice pudding, arrange on plates, and drizzle with the syrup. Serve immediately.

ROSIN'S TIP: Only marinate fruits in very flavorful liquids. Any liquid with a less concentrated flavor than the fruit leeches the taste from the fruit. Adding the juice of a ½ lemon gives the taste a boost.

RED PEPPER BUTTER CREAM SPONGE WITH MARINATED STRAWBERRIES

Everyone knows butter cream and sponge cake—but certainly not in combination with red bell pepper! Taste and be astonished is what I say about this extraordinary dessert.

> serves 4–6
> 2 hours + 4 hours to refrigerate

1 To make the sponge cake, preheat the oven to 350°F (170°C). Dry-roast the almonds in a frying pan until golden brown. Remove from the heat and let cool. Beat the eggs, egg yolk, and sugar for 10 minutes, until foamy. Sift the flour and cornstarch over the egg mixture and add the almonds. Fold all the ingredients together without forming any clumps. Line a 6 × 6in (15 × 15cm) baking pan with parchment paper. Pour the batter into the pan. Place the pan on the center rack of the oven and bake for 14–18 minutes, until the cake is done.

2 To make the red pepper butter cream, place the milk, vanilla seeds, sugar, and pudding powder in a saucepan and bring to a boil. Remove from the heat and cool. Stir in the egg yolks. Cover with plastic wrap and let cool. For Step 3, the vanilla cream, butter, and red pepper reduction must be at room temperature or the butter cream won't bind.

3 Sift the confectioners' sugar into a bowl, add the butter, and beat for 5 minutes, until foamy. Gradually beat in the pudding and red pepper reduction, alternating the two, until the butter cream is smooth. Spread the mixture evenly over the cake. Cover and refrigerate for 4 hours.

4 Before serving, zest and juice the lemon. Hull and quarter the strawberries, then season to taste with Grand Marnier, lemon juice, lemon zest, and honey. Remove the butter cake from the pan and cut it into 2in (5cm) cubes. Divide the strawberries among the cake pieces and serve.

SPONGE

1 cup sliced almonds
4 eggs
1 egg yolk
⅓ cup sugar
½ cup all-purpose flour
1 tsp cornstarch

RED PEPPER BUTTER CREAM

1½ cups milk
seeds of 2 vanilla pods
3 tbsp sugar
¼ cup vanilla pudding powder
2 egg yolks
½ cup confectioners' sugar
32 tbsp unsalted butter, at room temperature
⅔ cup red bell pepper reduction (see page 218)

STRAWBERRIES

1 organic lemon
10 strawberries
2 tsp Grand Marnier
1 drizzle of honey

BASIC RECIPES

BASIC RECIPES

Many of these salad dressings, sauces, and seasonings are available in supermarkets, but the flavor of homemade products is so much better than store-bought.

OIL AND VINEGAR DRESSING

2 cups vegetable stock / ¼ cup white wine vinegar / ¾ cup
   olive oil / sugar / salt / freshly ground black pepper

Place the vegetable stock in a saucepan and bring to a boil. Simmer until the stock becomes concentrated. Remove from the heat. Whisk in the vinegar. Using a handheld mixer, beat in the olive oil a bit at time. Season to taste with sugar, salt, and pepper.

MUSTARD DRESSING

½ cup red Port wine / ½ cup Madeira wine / 1 tbsp dry
   vermouth / ⅔ cup balsamic vinegar / 2 cups olive oil /
   1 tsp mustard / salt / sugar

Place the Port and Madeira in a saucepan and bring to a boil. Reduce the liquid to ½ cup. Add the dry vermouth and vinegar. Remove from the heat. Using a handheld blender, blend in the olive oil and the mustard a little at time. Season to taste with salt and sugar.

YOGURT DRESSING

1 garlic clove / 1¼ cups yogurt / ¼ cup heavy cream /
   ¼ cup white balsamic vinegar / juice of ½ lemon /
   ½ tsp honey / salt / freshly ground black pepper / sugar

Peel and chop the garlic. Using a handheld blender, blend together the yogurt, cream, and garlic. Add the balsamic vinegar, lemon juice, and honey and blend again. Season with salt, pepper, and sugar. Strain through a sieve.

CHAMPAGNE DRESSING

2 shallots / 1 garlic clove / ½ cup olive oil / sugar / salt /
   freshly ground black pepper / ⅔ cup vegetable stock /
   1 cup Champagne vinegar

Peel and dice the shallots and garlic. Heat a little olive oil in a saucepan. Add the shallots and garlic and sauté for 5 minutes, until translucent. Season with sugar, salt, and pepper. Add the stock. Bring to a boil. Remove from the heat and add the vinegar. Blend using a handheld blender. Gradually beat in the remaining olive oil. Strain through a sieve.

ELDERFLOWER DRESSING

2 shallots / 1 garlic clove / olive oil / salt / sugar /
   2 cups elderflower juice / ½ cup stock / ¼ cup white wine
   vinegar / ½ cup olive oil

Peel and dice the shallots and garlic. Heat 1 tablespoon of olive oil in a frying pan. Add the shallots and garlic and sauté until translucent. Season with salt and sugar. Continue to cook over medium heat for 2 minutes. Add the elderflower juice and reduce the liquid to 1 cup. Add the stock and vinegar. Remove from the heat and blend using a handheld blender. Work in the remaining olive oil a little at a time. Season to taste with salt and sugar. Strain through a sieve.

ROSIN'S TIP:

You can also use the remoulade right after the olive oil has been incorporated.

REMOULADE FOAM

1 shallot / ⅔ cup, plus 1 tbsp olive oil / 4 egg yolks / 2 tsp dill pickle liquid, from the jar / 1 tbsp mustard / 1 tbsp sugar / 1 tsp dried dill

Peel and dice the shallot. Heat 1 tablespoon of olive oil in a frying pan. Add the shallot, and sauté until translucent. Remove from the heat. Place the shallots, egg yolks, pickle liquid, mustard, sugar, and dill into a container. Blend using a handheld blender. Strain through a sieve. Slowly blend in ⅔ cup of olive oil until thick and creamy. Place the cream in an iSi-Whip and use 3 cream chargers. Warm in 160°F (70°C) hot water for 15 minutes. Shake well and foam.

MAYONNAISE

2 egg yolks / salt / 1 pinch of sugar / 1 tsp mustard / 1 pinch of cayenne pepper / 1 tbsp distilled vinegar / 1¾ cups canola oil

Using a whisk, combine all the ingredients except the oil in a metal bowl. Whisk in the oil very slowly in a thin stream until the mayonnaise is thick and creamy.

COCKTAIL SAUCE

½ cup mayonnaise (see recipe above) / 3 tbsp tomato paste / 1 splash of cognac / 2 tbsp lemon juice / salt / cayenne pepper

Place the mayonnaise, tomato paste, cognac, and lemon juice in a bowl and stir them together. Season to taste with salt and cayenne pepper.

TOMATO SALSA

4 tomatoes / 1 red onion / 1 tbsp apricot kernel oil or pumpkin seed oil / 1 tbsp chopped herbs (such as parsley and basil) / 1 tbsp aged balsamic vinegar / 1 tbsp olive oil / salt / freshly ground black pepper / sugar

Blanch the tomatoes in boiling water, remove the skins and seeds, and dice. Peel and dice the onion. Combine the apricot kernel oil or pumpkin oil, tomatoes, onion, herbs, balsamic vinegar, and olive oil. Season to taste with salt, pepper, and sugar. Marinate in the refrigerator for at least 1 hour before serving.

RED BELL PEPPER REDUCTION

12 red bell peppers / 2 stalks of lemongrass / ½ cup sugar / seeds of 1 vanilla bean / 10 Kaffir lime leaves / 5 cloves

Cut the peppers in half, remove the seeds and pith, chop them coarsely, and juice them in a juicer. You need 2½ cups of red bell pepper juice. Chop the lemongrass. Caramelize the sugar in a saucepan. Stir in the vanilla seeds, Kaffir lime leaves, lemongrass, and cloves. Add 2½ cups of red pepper juice. Reduce the liquid to ⅔ cup. Remove from the heat, strain through a sieve, and let cool.

VEGETABLE STOCK

2 carrots / 1 onion / 1 garlic clove / ½ head of celery root /
  1 bunch of parsley / 2 tbsp sunflower oil /
  3 bay leaves / 2 cloves / 10 peppercorns / salt

Chop the carrots, onion, garlic, celery root, and parsley.
Heat the sunflower oil in a saucepan. Sauté the
vegetables and spices for 5 minutes. Add 8½ cups
of lightly salted water, bring to a boil, and boil for
10 minutes. Strain the stock through a sieve into a
second saucepan. Place it on the stove and reduce the
stock to 4 cups. This should take about 20 minutes.

ROSIN'S TIP:

Freeze the stock in ice-cube
trays and then use as many
cubes of stock as you need.

CLARIFIED BUTTER

Clarified butter is also known as ghee. To make ghee,
melt 18 tablespoons of unsalted butter in a frying pan
over low heat, until the whey foams up. Do not let it
turn brown. Strain the butter through a sieve lined with
paper towels and pour it into a glass jar. Clarified
butter keeps in the fridge for 1 month.

BROWN BUTTER

Brown butter has a delicious, nutty, flavor. Melt 18
tablespoons of unsalted butter in a frying pan until
the whey foams up. Continue heating the butter until it
starts to brown and you can smell it. Strain the butter
through a sieve lined with paper towels and pour it
into a glass jar. Brown butter keeps in the fridge for
1 month.

HERBED SALT

¼ cup mixed herbs (such as marjoram, rosemary, thyme,
  savory, and oregano) /1 cup coarse sea salt

Use a mortar and pestle to crush the herbs. Mix them
with the sea salt. Leave the mixture, uncovered, in a
dry place for 2 days so that the moisture the salt draws
from the herbs can escape.

INDEX